From Stephen and Diana.

Birthday 28 December 2002.

PANDORA'S
DAUGHTERS

By the same author

Wayward Women:
A Guide to Women Travellers

Unsuitable for Ladies:
An Anthology of Women Travellers

Angels of Albion:
Women of the Indian Mutiny

Parrot Pie for Breakfast:
An Anthology of Women Pioneers

PANDORA'S DAUGHTERS

The Secret History of Enterprising Women

Jane Robinson

CONSTABLE · LONDON

Constable & Robinson Ltd
3 The Lanchesters
162 Fulham Palace Road
London W6 9ER
www.constablerobinson.com

First published in the UK by Constable,
an imprint of Constable & Robinson Ltd 2002

A copy of the British Library Cataloguing in Publication
data is available from the British Library

ISBN 0-09480-510-5

Printed and bound in the EU

To
Dr Hannah Mortimer,
my sister.

CONTENTS

ILLUSTRATIONS

ACKNOWLEDGEMENTS

People always assume that writing a book is a lonely business, and sympathize with me for those endless hours spent sitting at a desk with no one to talk to but the word-processor. On the contrary: while necessarily a solitary occupation, writing is anything but lonely. I keep such stimulating company, and shall miss these roaring girls enormously now the book is finished and they have to leave to make way for the next. My first thanks must go to them, for being so unpredictable and inspiring.

For more concrete help I am indebted to the staff of the many libraries and museums visited in Britain and America during the course of my research. I should particularly mention Aylesbury Reference Library the Bodleian Library in Oxford (chiefly the Upper Reading Room and Rhodes House), the British Library, the London Library and New York Public Library. I owe a special acknowledgement to Caroline and Stuart Schimmel for their customary generosity with information and hospitality, to Milbry Polk for her enthusiasm and expertise, and to those many people who came up with suggestions, ideas and memories when badgered by me at the various workshops and courses I've led to explore the lives and work of history's career women.

For ferreting out obscure books and unlikely characters I'm grateful to Denise Dyson, Diana Evans, Christina Jeffery, Howard Mather, Valerie Ruddock, Mary Shearer and Peter Taylor. For other invaluable help I should like to thank my agent Caroline Dawnay, my editor Carol O'Brien, with the Baldassarre (extended) family for their advice, Annabel Hardman for her encouragement, Richard and Edward James for their patience, my mother Helen Robinson, and – as ever – Bruce.

For permissions to use extracted material I thank the following: The Penguin Group UK for *The Book of the City of Ladies* by Christine de Pizan, translation © Rosalind Brown-Grant (1999); and *The Erotic Poems* by Ovid, translation © Peter Green (1982); 'Lily the Pink' (traditional), arranged and adapted by John Gorman, Roger McGough and Mike Grear © copyright 1968 Noel Gay Music Company Ltd, used by permission of Music Sales Ltd.; Mary Reibey letter, dated October 1972, (ref ML MSS 5934: CY reel 3181) as reproduced by Nance Irvine, original is held in the Mitchell Library, State Library of New South Wales; *Woman Defamed and Woman Defended: An Anthology of Medieval Texts*, edited by Alcuin Blamires with Karen Pratt and C.W. Marx © Alcuin Blamires 1992, by permission of Oxford University Press.

INTRODUCTION

IT IS NOT ALWAYS EASY to tell where ideas for a book come from. They tend to creep up on you, emerging first as swaying little seedlings of interest you might not even remember planting, and then, with any luck, flourishing into the sort of hardy, robust enthusiasm you need to carry you through two or three years of writing and research. I know exactly how this book began, though. It was the day a neighbour gave me a copy of Alfred Lord Tennyson's *The Princess*. Inevitably the first lines to catch my eye as I flicked through the poem were these:

> The soft and milky rabble of womankind.
> Poor weakling e'en as they are . . .[1]

I didn't take too much umbrage, having read and written enough about history's more spirited women by then to realize that Tennyson was only being fashionable. He was very much a poet of his time, after all. But what I did not expect was the echo, in my mind, of a far angrier response to this soppiest of couplets from a crowd of half-forgotten individuals I had been vaguely stowing away for future reference.

These rather urgent women were all people I had come across tangentially during previous research, whose strength of character and originality had particularly struck me, but who seemed otherwise entirely uncategorizable. What, for example, could a naval commander in the Persian Wars have in common with an alchemist of third-century Alexandria? A Dark Age Pope with an Orcadian wind-seller? Or a human cannonball in Westminster with the woman who ran for President of the United States? It was only in their sudden imagined reaction to being labelled so soft and milky and weak that I realized why they belonged together. They were all what one of them proudly called 'self-sustaining', or self-employed working women, earning a rewarding living in a variety of chosen and sometimes unprecedented occupations, long before the concept of the career woman came into currency, and in defiance (as far as I knew) of all the expectations of their age. A less soft and milky lot one could not hope to meet.

That's how it all started, then: as someone who had always assumed the glass ceiling to have been a permanent historical fixture, its height imperceptibly raised – or not – as the centuries progressed, I became fascinated by these apparently idiosyncratic characters busy working for themselves. I wanted not only to know more about them and the social climate in which they lived, but also to discover how many others there were operating similarly behind the scenes of orthodox women's history during the long, supposedly dependent years before the vote.

A contemporary of Tennyson, the writer Sarah Mytton Maury, summed up the cloyingly genteel Victorian attitude to enterprising women perfectly:

> I have long been a sufferer from the stupid and cruel prejudices of my country, which exclude all females who labour either with their fingers or with their heads, *for remuneration*, from the rank and privileges of gentlewomen. By

reason of these purse-proud and vulgar prejudices, I was condemned by a Father's pride, and a Mother's tenderness, to abstain from every effort which might have contributed to their comfort or my own, and from gratifying my own feelings of independence by being actively useful. A woman in England, in consequence of the highly artificial state of our society, who rises superior to the frowns of fortune, *in fact she who works*, is looked upon as degraded, as separated for ever from the class in which she was born; this false pride, and this abject fear of the loss of *caste*, warp and destroy the energies of many of my countrywomen.[2]

It *was* an artificial state of society, and it helped create a similarly artificial view of social history: so pungent and murky is the sanctimonious gloss with which the Victorians coated everything to do with women that we begin to suspect no ordinary female of any class can ever have achieved career success and remained respectable, no matter when she lived. That may be why I have found this book's women of enterprise so very exhilarating and attractive. They are irresistibly dynamic, supporting themselves and often others in startling, original ways, and driven by their particular circumstances and their own impulses far beyond the bounds of what we consider to be convention.

This book, in celebrating their unexpected exploits, spans some twenty-five centuries to the First World War, and although most of its subjects lived and worked in Britain or in North America, there are engineers from China, a spymaster from Japan, mountaineers and mercenaries in South America, war correspondents and gold-miners in South Africa, chemists and mathematicians from the Middle East, together with merchants and assorted entrepreneurs from all over Europe. I have avoided most of the occupations traditionally associated with women in order to concentrate on the really eccentric and colourful characters. After all, the only interesting women most histories throw up are those financially and educationally privileged enough to afford to be colourful. In the case of the women in this book, it is precisely because most of them had neither money (in the beginning) nor much schooling that they shone – and shine still.

Tennyson was not alone, of course, in lumping females together into some blancmangy mass: Western tradition has always had it that the weaker sex (with notable but lofty exceptions) was not allowed to be much else. Catherine Morland, in Jane Austen's *Northanger Abbey* (1818), used to complain that she found history deathly dull for just that reason: it was nothing but the 'quarrels of popes and kings, with wars or pestilences, in every page; the men all so good for nothing, and hardly any women at all . . .'[3] And it's true – if one subscribes to the easy over-generalization school of women's history, it becomes obvious that as soon as men could write about morality and society, women were utterly circumscribed.

The ladies encountered in history books (as opposed to biographies) have tended to be emblems or caricatures, famed for their mythical or mystical virtue, for their spiritual or temporal nobility, their wifely loyalty or motherly love, or their spectacular abandonment to the carnality of Eve. If they worked, then they were usually reduced to statistics: a certain percentage being domestic servants, another being peasants on the land, and others anonymously classed as assistants in their husband's business, weavers in the mills, factory labourers, match-girls, the odd midwife, the even odder maverick, and all those myriads of spinsters. Perhaps those fortunate souls able to take advantage of any education available as time went on might have flourished in the limited spheres such an education prescribed – as governesses, companions, teachers, nurses, and so on. Some might even have progressed beyond, pioneering in the male professions of medicine, politics, law and science, but if they did, they probably became 'unsexed' in the process, and so they never really counted as ladies at all.

I have always felt repelled by this anonymous treatment of women's history. Why should all women travellers, for instance, conform to the stereotypical image of an indomitable Victorian virgin, vigorously prodding the ends of the earth with a parasol and a vaguely disapproving air?[4] Or all suffragettes be considered shrill and strident, desperate for martyrdom and glory? And why should every so-called career woman be stylized as an over-ambitious and stony-hearted virago? It does seem a little unfair. So I have to admit that as well as being a chance for me to introduce some of the most spirited – even outrageous – characters I have ever come across, this book is also an attempt to knock down these stereotypes.

By writing it I wanted first to prove Tennyson and Catherine Morland wrong: an entertaining but not exactly difficult task, given the material. Then, by setting the achievements of my characters into their social, political and cultural contexts, I wanted to give an impression of the changing attitudes to working women through the past couple of millennia or so, and find out whether those attitudes had any bearing on individual working lives.

Lastly, I felt I owed it to these strong-minded individuals to lend them a voice again. Many seem to have been surprisingly undistinguished in their own time, and even those who were well known once may since have become swallowed up in a retrospective mêlée. The whole discipline of women's history could do with a few more *names*, personalities, and more individual panache . . . Enter Pandora's daughters.

1

PANDORA'S DAUGHTERS

I LIKE TO BEGIN CHAPTERS WITH QUOTATIONS. Not only does it look quite scholarly, but a pithy little epigram or couplet can illuminate nicely what follows. Anyone writing a book about people, like this one, should surely have a splendid supply of quotes at their disposal.

In fact, although there has been no problem in heading all the other chapters, for this opening one I have drawn a blank. The reason is quite simple: during the period it covers, from antiquity to the end of the first millennium, you can hardly hear a woman's voice at all. In fact, sometimes it is difficult for an historian to believe that Western women were capable of independent movement before about AD 1400. For all the shadowy centuries before, looming out of prehistory and reaching towards the Renaissance, the females of the world are more like cut-out shapes, propelled around their age by unseen hands. They tend to come on in the crowd scenes, as noblewomen, nuns, peasants or slaves; even if they are named, like queens and saints, they are merely representations of power (someone else's) and morality (God's). They live undeveloped, labelled lives, as passive foils to men's activity. And they certainly don't speak sense.

They don't even think, according to received wisdom (which ought always to be treated with suspicion). The very word 'woman' in Latin (*mulier*) is said to derive from *mollities mentis*, meaning soft-minded.[1] Instead of thinking, they react, and are always woefully true to type: a substantial body of the literature surviving from the eighth century BC to the Middle Ages, when it considers woman at all, has her either as the temptress, who excites a man into betraying himself and his God through lust and cupidity, or the scold, who punishes him for his human imperfections (inherited, of course, from his mother's side). This little medley illustrates the point:

> Countless are the traps which the scheming enemy [i.e. the devil] has set throughout the world's paths and plains: but among them the greatest – and the one scarcely anybody can evade – is woman. Woman the unhappy source, evil root, and corrupt offshoot, who brings to birth every sort of outrage throughout the world. For she instigates quarrels, conflicts, dire dissensions; she provokes fighting between old friends, divides affections, shatters families ... She hurls conflagration as she rampages through farmsteads and fields. In sum, there lurks in the universe no manifestation of evil in which woman does not claim some part for herself.
>
> *Bishop Marbod of Rennes*[2]

No novelty, either, about the cause of warfare. Europe
   And Asia would never have been
Embroiled without Helen's abduction ...
     ... A woman, Lavinia, got the
   Trojans fighting again, for the second time,
     When they set foot on Latin soil. While our city was
      still new-founded
Those Sabine girls screaming rape

[2]

Provoked most bloody reprisals. I've seen two bulls
   battling
Over a snow-white heifer – she egged them on.

Ovid[3]

From garments cometh a moth, and from a woman the
iniquity of man . . .

Ecclesiasticus 42:13[4]

A woman's chastity consists in not being asked.

Ovid[5]

All that reminds me of the cartoon where a man fantasizes of
the balloon-bosomed bimbo he left behind in the pub while
lurching home to his lantern-jawed wife who waits with a raised
rolling-pin. The two types – temptress and scold – are alive and
kicking still.

Too long obscured by the easy appeal of caricature is an
altogether more intriguing narrative: the story of those women
who defied, or more often simply ignored, the expectations of
their age. The self-supporting women I am concerned with did
not necessarily want, need or know how to make a statement
about their work, and there is little wonder that their era can seem
like a succession of scenes in a puppet theatre. Few contemporary
authors wrote about individual women living particular lives,
and throughout ancient history there was a vigorous tradition
of goddesses and mythical mortals whose glamorous adventures
and significance eclipsed reality.

The deeper back into time you go, the more powerful these
goddesses become. The Greek Gaia was the earth herself, who bore
and nurtured everything that grew. She embraced the whole of
creation. The Egyptian mother-goddess Isis is credited with being
her people's first lawyer, who taught them how to write, to pray, to
embalm their dead, and to build and navigate their boats on the

[3]

River Nile. Ishtar did much the same for the Assyrians. Athene, or Minerva, is well known in the cabinet of the gods as minister for wisdom and war, but she also held responsibility for agriculture (inventing the plough, the yoke and the bridle); she was the first to press olive oil from a fruit she had designed herself, and she even fashioned the first flute, although she was not, she admitted, a musician.

The rot set in with Athene's daughter Pandora, and with that other mother of mankind, Eve, who I shall come to later on.

At school, Pandora always struck me as one of Olympus's more spirited creations.[6] Commissioned (from the blacksmith) by Zeus to punish Prometheus's wayward humans for indulging in the gift of fire, she danced into life after a kiss from Athene, and enchanted all who saw her – gods and mortals alike – with her brilliance and love of life. Zeus endowed her with all the talents he could muster (the most lethal, he said, being the ability to speak), and a jar (her 'box') to deliver to her chosen husband, Prometheus's brother, Epimetheus. In return, Zeus exacted a promise from Pandora never to open the jar herself.

Down tripped Pandora to earth, where she immediately met Epimetheus, captivated (or ensnared) him with her persuasive words and body, and prepared to hand over her dowry. But having been given all the gifts (as her name suggests), including intelligence and inquisitiveness, she could not resist opening the jar herself – just a little – to see what its secret consignment could be. First a bee meandered out and stung her nose. Then a dog fought free and bit her husband, and then chaos ensued. Zeus had shut away all the evils of the world in that jar; he knew the woman he had created could be relied upon to unleash them on a deserving world. The job was done, and Prometheus's puny people were condemned.

But there was a codicil to the story, and this is what appealed so much to me as a child. While the fumes of hatred and disease were still shimmering above an apparently empty jar, the mortified

Pandora noticed something floundering about at the bottom. She looked inside and there was a small bird struggling to escape. She coaxed it up and it settled on her finger before flying off uncertainly into the future. It was hope.

All this, like the story of Eve, is supposed to be about temptation, punishment, weakness, guilt, and so on. The Greek poet Hesiod (*fl.* eighth century BC) was explicit in his interpretation of the myth, calling Pandora a 'lovely curse', from whom sprang 'all womankind, the deadly female race and tribe of wives who live with mortal men and bring them harm.'[7] But my naive childhood reading of it was quite different. I saw Pandora as a heroine, beautiful and beloved; the one who had the courage to defy the pompous gods and the patience to wait comfortingly by man's side for the good things once the bad had passed away. She appeared far more positive a character than poor, soiled Eve: Pandora's disobedience was a matter of healthy curiosity, whereas Eve's has acquired a gloss of feebleness and shame.

Pandora was not exactly self-sustaining, however: she may have supported the entire female race, but she did not, as far as I know, go out into the world and earn an independent living. There are other appealing characters from ancient history whose lives – real and imagined – may have come a little closer to the remit of this book. The barbaric tribe of Amazons, for example, said to be a mercenary band of warriors from south-west Asia, were ruthless and predatory, so dedicated to the art of killing that each hacked off her own right breast the better to draw her bow, and, as one of my sources puts it, 'not generally sympathetic to men.'[8]

Moving away from the mythical, there are records of Egyptian women working as scribes and astronomers, or attending schools of medicine, during the third millennium BC.[9] Two Sumerian businesswomen flourished during the following millennium in the perfume industry, according to cuneiform inscriptions: one was a chemical engineer named Tapputi-Belatekallim,[10] and the other (only part of whose name survives) was described as a perfume factory foreman or supervisor. Pliny said that it was a woman who first picked and processed cotton (Pamphile of Cea); Boccaccio credited Queen Ceres of Sicily (rather than Athene) with the invention of the plough and the first production of leavened bread. He also claimed the Asian Arachne of Colophon as the first to think of making nets – so fiendishly clever an idea that the gods grew jealous and turned her into a spider. These women are all rather blurred and distant, however, and it is not until about 500 BC that my characters shift more clearly into focus, operating as independent people against a somewhat more clearly defined and documented background.

Artemisia of Halicarnassus (c.484–c.430 BC) features in the *Histories* of Herodotus as a heroine of the Persian Empire during its wars against the Greeks.[11] She was queen of the city now known as Bodrum in Turkey, a powerful widow, and an inveterate adventurer. Well aware of the Persians' intended invasion of Greece in 480 BC, she furnished their King Xerxes with five fully equipped triremes,[12] amongst 'the most famous ships in the fleet',[13] and insisted on commanding one of them herself: '[even] though she had now a son grown up . . . her brave spirit and manly daring sent her forth to the war, when no need required her . . .' As Xerxes' armoured admiral she engaged her fleet in the battle of Salamis as ruthlessly as any Amazon, once saving herself from the pursuing Greek enemy by hastily hiding her ensign and ramming another Persian ship as a decoy. This was hailed not as treachery, but the finest display of naval tactics: Artemisia was quite simply 'the only person who knew what was best to be done.'

It was as the king's counsellor of war, however, that she really gained his – and Herodotus's – respect: when circumstances allowed she was quick (and courageous) to argue against over-aggression and for strategic prudence, once warning rather archly that the Greek navy was as far superior to the Persian 'as men are to women'. Whether he took her advice or not, Xerxes acknowledged that any success he enjoyed was due largely to Artemisia, for at sea 'my men have behaved like women,' he said, but 'my women have behaved like men.'

Artemisia was a queen, of course, and no queen needs a career. But Herodotus makes the point that she chose to go to sea, and she would certainly have been well rewarded for her heroism. Other sources hint at her managing a highly successful piracy enterprise:[14] this was a woman who knew her place – and ignored it.

Or perhaps there was no such concept then of a woman knowing her place? Perhaps women had always done what they could, according to their circumstances rather than their gender? Think of the Sumerian chemists, or of the renowned women engineers of ancient China.[15] A picture found in a tomb in the Valley of the Kings records the female 'Chief Physician' Merit Ptah (*fl. c.*2700 BC),[16] and Pharaoh Rameses III (1197–1167 BC) issued an inscription stating his pride at enabling 'the woman of Egypt to go her own way, her journeys being extended where she wanted, without any person assaulting her on the road'.[17] Egyptian women – if free – had more legal rights and privileges than either the Greeks or the Romans. Yet even the Greeks could celebrate the odd mortal woman occasionally. Theano of Croton (in southern Italy) was one of them.

Theano (*fl. c.*500 BC) was a student of the mathematician Pythagoras, then his wife, and finally, as his widow, the leader of his community of philosophers and intellectuals. She is supposed to have written treatises on number theory, on physics and medicine, and even child psychology; her daughters Damo, Arignote and Myia all contributed to the family canon of works on philosophy, mathematics and behavioural science. Myia especially advocated temperance (for a woman) in all things, harmony and balance being as important in the human and spiritual being as in the animal and metaphysical worlds. It is a theory Plato (427–347 BC) might have shared: his *Republic* allowed women – a complementary species

[7]

to man – to be individuals, educated and guardians of the general good. They should inspire men and bear their children with pride (leaving men themselves to make love on a higher plane to the goddess Knowledge and sire wisdom and ideas). A fine theory, wrote Plato, worthy of Utopia, but unfortunately impractical in the real world. There, however much freedom and teaching might be offered to women, nothing they could ever think or do would better men. They were just not made that way.

Plato's pupil Aristotle (384–322 BC) went further. To him, men and women were not separate species, but analogues of the same one. His females are damaged, mutant males. They menstruate because their blood has not been properly 'cooked', and so weakly dribbles out of their malformed and unfinished bodies. Their humour is too cold to distil semen (the essence of the human soul); their mind is watery and capricious, their body all matter and no movement, and their soul no more than the vaguest reflection of a man's. (One wonders, incidentally, where this leaves Aristotle's wife, the distinguished marine zoologist and scientific author Pythias of Assos . . .)[18]

And so we begin to cross the Rubicon: as soon as men's analyses of women were written down with authority, and so taught (to men) and articulated around the civilized world of Greece and Rome, then those women became defined and thus circumscribed. The more rhetorical these commentators were, the less sentient seemed their subject, until eventually, fuelled by early Christendom's spokesmen, this 'two-legged she-beast' grew to represent all that men had ever been ashamed of, and all they most resented.

The apotheosis of this highly structured misogyny was still to come in Jean de Meun's *The Romance of the Rose* (AD 1275); meanwhile, of course, ordinary lives were being led by men and women, ignorance being (qualified) bliss. I refuse to believe that independent spirits flourish only when there is someone around to record them, but sadly we have no way of knowing, until a good few centuries later, how the more adventurous of *private* women chose to support themselves. Instead, we read that the average girl of Athens led an impotent and secluded life. She was legislated into near-oblivion and surfaced only as a slave, a prostitute, as goods on the marriage market, or a cultish priestess or seer. When we see her depicted on vases, amphorae, friezes and the like, she's demurely spinning or weaving, seducing or being seduced, fetching water, playing the harp, occasionally disguised titillatingly as a man, or striding vaingloriously about as an Amazon. That is as close to her private life as we get. None of her legislators and chroniclers, and surely few of her illustrators, would be women themselves; real mothers, daughters and sisters would be too busy getting themselves and their families through the day to be aware of what was being prescribed or denied them by the ruling intelligentsia.

Roman matrons, especially during the Empire (27 BC–AD 476), appear to have had a slightly more cheerful time, with growing legal recognition, social standing and religious influence, and there is a homely grace about their murals and mosaics lacking in the altogether more stylized illustrations of the Greeks. We glimpse a vignette of a girl thoughtfully sucking a stylus and patently wondering what to write next, for example, or another confidently measuring drops from a phial into a crucible: perhaps the first was a professional scribe? Or the second an apothecary? It is so tempting to appropriate images like these and turn them into portraits of distant, unknown career women, especially in this period of women's history when hard evidence scarcely exists. Then we come to the fourth century AD, and a city more vibrant and liberal than Athens or Rome – Alexandria.

Given its industrial and cultural provenance, it should be no surprise that Alexandria proved so supportive of early scientists. Perfumes and aromatic oils had been concocted and distilled there for generations; cosmetic and jewellery businesses flourished, with the parallel research and development of artificial gems; artists in a variety of media learned how to mix dyes and tint metals and cloth. And many of its citizens enjoyed comparative religious freedom and mutual respect, be they Copt or Gnostic, Greek or Jew, Christian, or even female. Alexandria, during the first few hundred years of the first millennium AD, was a highly stimulating place in which to live and work.

The alchemists Maria the Jewess and Cleopatra of Alexandria doubtless found it so. Their science of transmuting base materials into bullion, combining exotic and esoteric arts with scientific and philosophical method, must have seemed irresistibly fitting for such a rich and promising city. At the time they were practising, metallurgy and chemistry were only just emerging from the realms of the occult. Various metals were still considered either male or female, and the nature of their alloy depended on the manner of their consummation. An alchemist needed research skills, a means of precise measurement, the right equipment with which to experiment, and the intuition necessary to persuade materials to fuse and be fruitful: a mixture of theory, practice and faith.

Maria the Jewess concentrated on the equipment. In the fragments of her work that survive in *Maria Practica*,[19] she describes various of her inventions, including a three-armed still, a hot ash-bath and, for a gentler heat, a fermenting 'dung bed'. There is a special palette, too, for heating metals to a paste and colouring them with pigments, but her most famous piece of apparatus, still used by alchemists of a different kind today, is a water-bath designed to change the temperature – and the nature – of ingredients very, very gradually. It is known, of course, as a *bain-marie*.

Maria was a specialist, but her probable contemporary, Cleopatra of Alexandria, was the complete alchemist. A single papyrus page of her definitive text *Chrysopoeia* (*Goldmaking*) survives, displaying an array of diagrams and symbols with an inscription of virtuosic abstrusity: 'One is the Serpent, which has its poison according to two compositions, and One is All, and through it is All, and by it is All, and if you have not All, All is Nothing.'

From students of her work (which remained available in

successive manuscripts until the eleventh century) we learn that Cleopatra was reassuringly practical, too. She was one of the first scientists to realize and record the significance of quantifying experimental materials, and of accurate weight and measurement in the laboratory. Both she and Maria should have died rich and satisfied (but then, so should every successful alchemist).

The alchemists of Alexandria were highly educated men and women. Indeed, of all the times and places covered in this book, it is hard to think of another so supportive of women scholars. Come the cusp of the fourth and fifth centuries AD, however, the shutters were cranking down even there. The waning Roman Empire, newly converted to Christianity, was zealously engaged in a power struggle which equated religious difference with political dissent. Experimental science and philosophy became seditious paganism and heresy, and liberality towards women signalled corruption and moral decay.

Against this inauspicious background worked Hypatia (c.355–415), writer and university lecturer on mathematics, astronomy, philosophy and mechanics. Hypatia's father, Theon, was himself an eminent mathematician and philosopher; he relished his daughter's academic appetite and declared that in her he had created the perfect person. She certainly seems to have been modest and loyal, as well as charismatic, highly principled (vowing to be wed only to 'the truth') and intellectually rigorous. She gathered about her a community – almost a college – of like-minded Neoplatonists, attracted to the university by her inspirational public lectures and to her home by the private seminars and tutorials she gave. All were welcome. Students (looking to the Romans suspiciously like acolytes) travelled from Syria and Constantinople to hear her; they called her a 'blessed lady', their 'divine guide', and declared that the beauty of her mind was matched only by that of her body and soul.

The closest account we have of Hypatia and her work comes from the letters of one of these students, Synesius of Cyrene.

Sadly only his half of their correspondence survives, all Hypatia's own writing being destroyed after her death, but her originality, enthusiasm and generosity are all obvious – which makes her end all the more distressing.

Scholars argue about the precise motives for Hypatia's murder. Some say it was a political affair to do with her friendship with Orestes, one of Alexandria's civil leaders opposed to the Christian patriarch Cyril; others maintain she was a victim of Cyril's religious bigotry. Hypatia embraced political incorrectness, being tolerant – even defensive – of all rationally held beliefs; her celebrated facility with numbers smacked of cabalism, and her open-mindedness was no doubt dangerously infectious. To put it crudely, she was one of the most influential pagans in – and beyond – Alexandria. And a woman, too.

Whatever the real reason, in March 415, when she would have been about sixty, a mob of Cyril's most fanatical followers intercepted Hypatia outside the Caesarium church in the city; they pulled her from her chariot, dragged her into the church, stripped her, and proceeded to scour the flesh from her bones with oyster shells and shards of pottery until she was dead. Her body was then quartered, removed from the church, and burned to dust.[20]

The Dark Ages had arrived.

The darkness did not descend all at once, however. The queens and the saints were still regularly being shuffled on and off the stage, but there was an increasing number of sacred and secular women in the background ministering to the very young, the very old, or the very weak. Only a widow or virgin would be appointed to any sort of public work; if not a nun, she might be a nurse, for example, in Fabiola's hospital in Ostia,[21] or an ordained deaconess (providing she was over the age of forty) in the Byzantine East.

A woman might travel – even write about it – like Egeria the Blessed,[22] an abbess sent from her community in Spain to make pilgrimage to Jerusalem in 381. Egeria was an indomitable character, a scholar, whose dearest dream was to track the wanderings of the Israelites which, using the book of Exodus as her guide, she did. She lived in Jerusalem for a while, made an ascent of Mount Sinai, and wrote wonderfully vigorous letters home ('lovely ladies, light of my heart, you *know* how inquisitive I am . . .') describing all she saw and felt.

Some of Egeria's Pandoric spirit may be glimpsed in the Byzantine Empress Theodora (497–548): they share a strength of character and self-confidence rarely allowed common women at the time. Theodora was the daughter of the man who kept the bears at the Constantinople Hippodrome, and when orphaned at the age of four, she progressed from the circus to the theatre, working first as a dresser, and then as a dancer, mime artist and comic. She was deservedly popular, but life as an entertainer discontented her, and when a lover – the Byzantine equivalent of a minor civil servant – was posted to Cyrene in North Africa, she decided to go too. It is a mark of her confidence that she left this lover soon afterwards, and took herself back to Constantinople, travelling through Egypt and somehow gathering herself an education en route.

When Justinian first met her, she was living as a wool-spinner in the city; so besotted did they become with one another that he promptly passed a new law in order to allow them to marry, across what would before have been an unnegotiable social divide. When he became Emperor in 527, Theodora sat at his side as Empress.

Justinian and Theodora presided in partnership over one of Constantinople's most constructive periods. The Empress was a consummate politician: cannily prefacing her projects with an apology for venturing, as a woman, to talk at all, she went on to reform and develop the city and its people – especially its women – in a radically original way. She was responsible for humanistic changes in legislation affecting religious minorities, women's inheritance and dowry issues, and divorce. She passionately believed in the rights of the individual, deeming

[13]

pimps and brothel-keepers to be criminals, and freeing girls sold into prostitution – by buying their liberty herself, if necessary. Children were absolved the responsibility of their parents' debts (thus avoiding the obligation to be sold into slavery). While she actively concerned herself in the moral and physical welfare of her weaker subjects, she kept a sage and constant watch on the political machinations of the strong.

In this age, as in others, there must have been so many more women like her: ordinary women, bursting with vitality and passion and wisdom, but with no hope, because of their circumstances, of blossoming. What happened to these women? Did they all die frustrated? Or did they get on and adventure, unrecorded, as best they could? There is always folklore, of course, and it makes sense to consider crediting those women celebrated in legend and anecdote with some foundation in fact.

So far, most of the women we have come across were renowned as much for their virtuosity as their gender. Artemisia was an accomplished naval commander; Maria and Cleopatra were distinguished alchemists; and Hypatia is remembered for her intellect and influence. All of them, including Egeria and Theodora, were remarkable people, not just remarkable women. That is a legacy of their historical distance and their comparatively unarticulated position in society: even given the claims of Aristotle and Ovid, the codes of Roman law, and the strictures of the Bible, the inherent disability of women was not yet universally ratified.

Pope Joan now presents a different picture. She is notorious solely because of her sex. Had she never been discovered, her impact on Vatican history would probably have been minimal. As it is, she looms embarrassingly large; perhaps even larger than life.

As the first Christian millennium progressed, women worked – and were seen to be working – in a number of respectable professions. Increasingly, though, these professions tended to be linked to the Church, or to charity. By the time Pope Joan was born, in about 820, it was natural for a good woman (virgin, wife, or widow)[23] to choose the house of her father, of her husband, or of God in which to do her duty (and whatever she did, she must do it *dutifully*). She might even be so virtuous that she transcended her blighted gender altogether. As St Jerome put it, in her natural state, bearing and caring for children, a woman is as different from a man as the body is from the soul (a woman being, essentially, the body, and the man, the soul). 'But when she wishes to serve Christ more than the world, then she will cease to be a woman and will be called man.'[24] How better to describe an unconventional yet irreproachable female than as an honorary male? That is how Xerxes explained Artemisia's valour, after all.

Exceptional women might aspire to bleach out the stain of original sin, just as Christ's mother Mary was able to do, with piety. Monasteries and convents stood side by side, with the abbess as venerable – and innovative, sometimes – as the abbot. Certainly St Hilda of Whitby shone amongst her contemporaries in the seventh century as a spiritual authority and advisor, and Lioba of Wimborne (*c.*700–80) was famed as a learned evangelist of her faith. In fact Lioba was a traveller, too: in 748 she led a mission of nuns 'shoulder to shoulder' from Britain and Ireland on a perilous journey to the poor, benighted Teutons of present-day Germany.

Amongst those missionaries who followed in Lioba's footsteps some decades later (or so we are told) was a young English couple – presumably lay people – whose daughter, Joan, was born at either Mainz or Fulda. Joan was allowed to attend the local monastery school until she was twelve; soon afterwards she continued her education herself by running away with a fellow scholar (or monk, or lover, or teacher, or all three) and settling down at university in Athens.[25] Historical sources are less than definite on the exact course of Joan's life, hence the alternatives available at crucial points. It may be that she travelled as a holy woman, but it is more likely that for liberty's sake she lived outwardly as a monk during this period. Clerical habits were dark and voluminous, and a convenient vogue had only recently resulted in papal orders for priests to be clean-shaven.

What happened to Joan's companion we do not know. She progressed to Rome, however, and is supposed to have taught at a Greek school on the Aventine Hill. Her public lectures there, like Hypatia's in Alexandria, attracted the notice of the great and the good, with the staggering result that in the year 855, 'Joan of England', aged about thirty-five, was elected Pope John VIII.

Scholars have run riot with the story ever since. There is no authentic mention of Pope Joan until 1265; thereafter claims and counter-claims are hurled across the centuries by Catholic apologists and their accusers. The former claim the whole story was a Protestant conspiracy, aimed at ridiculing the papacy, or else that Joan was the anti-Christ, the whore of the Apocalypse, sent unsuccessfully by Satan to turn the world upside down. The Protestants, joined later by feminists, reply that there is every reason to believe that Joan did exist, and that by becoming Pope she (a) proved a peerless cipher for papal corruption, or (b) followed her vocation, and died a martyr. The proof, they say, is to be found on the streets of Rome, where a statue of her is known to have existed in 1375 between the Colosseum and St Clement's Basilica, noted with surprise by Martin Luther in 1510, and removed at the end of the sixteenth century. There is a street, the via Sacra, which before Joan's time was part of the route taken by papal processions but afterwards – for reasons which will become obvious – was renamed and carefully avoided. And in the Vatican now there stands a gloomy-looking throne of plum-coloured porphyry with a hole in the seat, like a commode. For 600 years it was traditional that each pope (again, after Joan's time) sat there during his consecration while some diligent deacon or other, crouching on the floor, slid a hand underneath and through the hole to check his manhood. The Church did not want to make the same mistake twice.

Pope Joan's reign did not last long. For two years she appeared to conduct herself with probity and commitment to the job, but during an official procession in 858 her cover was spectacularly and irredeemably blown when, just as she reached the via Sacra (now via S. Giovanni), she gave birth.

It was the clerical equivalent of Pandora's box: all hell broke loose. Joan was dragged away and, with her bastard stillborn baby in her arms, taken outside the city walls and stoned to death. All official mention of her reign was immediately expunged from the chronicles, but the legend, as they say, lives on.

I suggested at the beginning of this chapter that although there is plenty written about women in general, it is difficult to find documentary evidence of individuals leading particular lives; after Joan, during the period between the ninth and twelfth centuries, the darkest of the Dark Ages, it becomes almost impossible. Only the odd tantalizingly ephemeral glimpse remains of the sort of independent soul this book is about. I should love to know more about the gynaecologist Trotula of Salerno (died *c.*1097), for example, whose text *De Passionibus Mulierum Curandorum* shows such a commonsensical approach to the treatment of women's and children's diseases. Copies still exist of this text, also known as *Trotula Major*: it became a standard work for training doctors up until the sixteenth century. But what of the woman herself? This passage from the book's prologue hints at her philosophy:

> Since then women are by nature weaker than men it is reasonable that sicknesses more often abound in them, especially around the organs involved in the work of nature. Since these organs happen to be in a retired location, women on account of modesty and the fragility and delicacy of the state of these parts dare not reveal the difficulties of their sicknesses to a male doctor. Wherefore I, pitying their misfortunes and at the

instigation of a certain matron [who?], began to study carefully the sicknesses which most frequently trouble the female sex.[26]

We know that the first medical school unattached to the Church flourished at Salerno during Trotula's time, and that she was by no means the only woman to study and teach there, 'the ladies of Salerno' being a recognized sorority of doctors. But did Trotula have her own list in the family medical practice? Did she, as a surgeon, use the methods she described so carefully in her own writing? Was she allowed to charge and manage her own fees?

And then there is St Euphrosyne of Polotsk (died 1173), in what is now Belarus. She is said to have copied and sold manuscripts for charity, but did she support herself too? Where and why was she granted an education?

As the centuries progress, of course, it becomes easier to assemble the working lives of individual women, and to shift some long-due attention from the paper figures of the puppet theatre to those people busy working behind the scenes.

Before doing that, though, we must not forget Eve. Just as images of real lives dimmed during the run-up to the Renaissance, so Eve became startlingly more visible. Most of the women in this book were familiar with her as the traitor of humanity; she was the pattern of them all. If they could read it, the Bible could tell them so; if not, their priest's interpretation of the scriptures would no doubt make it plain. They learned that having betrayed both God and her husband – heaven and earth – their mother Eve had bequeathed them an everlasting atonement of pain (in childbirth) and of subjection. The early Church Father Tertullian (160–225) was unequivocal:

The judgement of God upon [your] sex lives on in this age; therefore, necessarily the guilt should live on also. You are the gateway of the devil; you are the one who unseals the curse of that tree, and you are the one who persuaded [man] whom the devil was not capable of corrupting; you easily destroyed the image of God, Adam. Because of what you deserve, that is, death, even the Son of God had to die. And so you still think of adorning yourself above and beyond your tunics of animal skin? . . . Do you not know that you are Eve?[27]

Woman would never be free of the Devil: having tempted her once, he would prey on her always, looking for chinks in her lamentably flimsy armour, and taking swift advantage of every moral lapse.

The message was rammed home in other, more immediate, ways. Written or spoken words, however graphic, can rarely have been as eloquent to the ordinary (illiterate) man or woman as the gaudy and explicit picture on the lectern or church wall. And in St John's College in Cambridge there is a painting of the Temptation of Adam and Eve that conveys this powerfully.[28] In it, Eve is standing blatantly naked and self-assured (no fig-leaves or swathes of gauze here); between her and Adam is the tree of knowledge, around which coils Satan's smiling serpent with a coiffed and head-dressed human face. The serpent has hands: one has just given Eve the apple (which Eve in turn is offering Adam with a level gaze); the other is extended, and meets Eve's, palm to palm, like a secret symbol of conspiracy. Adam looks unsure and perplexed, but Eve is confident. Because the serpent is a woman, too.

2

FAR ABOVE RUBIES

Sick at heart . . . I thought myself very unfortunate that He
had given me a female form.

Christine de Pizan[1]

MEANWHILE – AND IT'S NICE TO THINK someone was counting
– a quarter of all new saints created between 1250 and 1300
were women.[2] Between 1400 and 1450, the figure rose to 30 per
cent, and a third of all ladies canonized between the thirteenth
and fifteenth centuries had not even been virgins when they
perished. Such spiritual generosity on the part of the Church
suggests that deeply dyed in iniquity as she was (and that picture
in St John's College shows just how deeply), Eve's stranglehold
on her daughters was slowly beginning to loosen at last.

As usual, there is no clear-cut division in history between the
world of the she-serpent and that of the real and possibly virtuous
woman. In fact, for much of the medieval period the two spin
self-contained and parallel. It is hard, after all, to put a date
on the birth of humanism, the beginning of the Renaissance,
and the invention of the female soul. Back in the early twelfth
century, Bishop Marbod of Rennes was able to write, with

impassioned conviction, that of all things 'seen to have been bestowed through God's gift to the advantage of humanity, we consider nothing to be more beautiful or better than a good woman'.[3] But almost in the same breath, he tells his readers that not only does woman (in general) subvert the world, but that she is the personification of 'sweet evil, compound of honeycomb and poison, spreading honey on her sword to transfix the hearts of the wise'.[4]

And he continues in the same vein:

> What is Woman? – Man's undoing; an insatiable animal; perpetual trouble and non-stop combat; man's daily ruin; a storm in the home; an impediment to peace of mind; the wreck of a weak-willed man; instrument of adultery; expensive war; the very worst creature and heaviest burden; fatal snake; [and most chilling of all:] human property.[5]

The theologian St Thomas Aquinas (1225–74) joined in by coolly declaring women to be a mistake, concluding that they 'ought not to have been produced in the original production of things. For [Aristotle] says that the female is a male *manqué*. But nothing *manqué* or defective should have been produced in the first establishment of things, so woman ought not to have been produced . . .'[6] He went on to discuss St Gregory's doctrine that 'where we have done no wrong we are all equal', and St Augustine's, that activity (i.e. the male estate) is always more honourable than passivity (the female). Women are to men as nature is to culture. Their bodies are their husband's while their spirits are the Lord's. Muslim tradition has it that women are the slates on which men write the history of the world: they are the instruments, and men make the music.

Then there is the single most influential literary work of the age: *The Romance of the Rose*, an epic, allegorical narrative begun relatively mildly in about 1240 by Guillaume de Lorris and completed some thirty-five years – and 18,000 aspersive lines – later by Jean de Meun. It tells a story set in a beautiful walled garden, where, like Eden, nothing unseemly is allowed through the gates. Outside may be clamouring the grotesque (and, incidentally, female) figures of Hatred, Avarice and Old Age, but they cannot come in. Only the fine young fellow who narrates the story is allowed to enter, because he is engaged on the noblest secular pursuit of all: the pursuit of Love. Love is a precious rosebud hidden in the garden, guarded by an ugly old woman; what our hero must do is seek out the rose and, with it, true happiness and fulfilment. He has some help on his mission: he meets 'Friend', who teaches him the art of seduction; then 'Genius' pleasurably impresses on him the importance of consummating desire in order to help Nature carry on her work. These are lessons gladly learned, and despite a path strewn by Jean de Meun with women's wiles and stupidity, and an ever-growing audience of siren-like figures luring the lover towards baser rewards than his chivalry demands, the flower is found, and plucked.

But the rose is decidedly sick: she is revealed as a 'lady slut', a 'vile bitch', not worth the winning:

> for no female will ever be so knowledgable, or be so firm-hearted, so steadfast or serious, that one could ever be sure of possessing her, never mind the trouble one took, any more than if one caught an eel by the tail in the Seine.[7]

Perhaps we have reached a turning point here: the point where those parallel worlds of devil and angel women began to turn towards each other, and the truth. *The Romance of the Rose* sums up the misogynistic tradition so far. It is lavish, cleverly wrought, fashionable and influential. But it is also provocative, and in a way I'm not sure its authors would have foreseen. It sparked off

[23]

a literary and eventually an ethical, humanist discussion, known as the 'Querelle' – the great dispute – which lasted well into the fifteenth century, and resulted (ironically, given the subject matter) in women speaking in their own defence louder and stronger than ever before.

So the climate gradually changed by degrees, and despite various elegant theological, philosophical and literary rantings, the possibility emerged during the Renaissance that perhaps women might *choose* how to behave. That they might even (given the chance) behave well – hence that avatar of sparkling new saints in the medieval heaven. Eve's dismal and damning pattern began to give way to more uplifting influences, selected from a wider variety of texts – and from living, or once living, exemplars.

The ultimate biblical role model was inevitably the Virgin Mary, but if she was a little too lofty, then perhaps Mary Magdalene would do. The latter was a penitent sinner, a woman who overcame her inherent corruption through recognition, atonement and service. She is like the woman 'far above rubies' in the book of Proverbs:

> The heart of her husband doth safely trust in her, so that he shall have no need of spoil. She will do him good and not evil all the days of her life. She seeketh wool, and flax, and worketh willingly with her hands. She is like merchant's ships; she bringeth her food from afar. She riseth also while it is yet night, and giveth meat to her household . . . She considereth a field, and buyeth it: with the fruit of her hands, she planteth a vineyard . . . She maketh fine linen, and selleth it; and delivereth girdles unto the merchant. Strength and honour are her clothing; and she shall rejoice in time to come. She openeth her tongue with wisdom; and in her tongue is the law of kindness . . . Her children arise up, and call her blessed; her husband also, and he praiseth her . . . Give her the

fruit of her hands; and let her own works praise her in the gates.[8]

This passage was translated from the Hebrew into Latin by St Jerome, in his Vulgate Bible, in the fifth century, and then into English by John Wycliffe in the 1380s. It is like a window on reality as far as I'm concerned: cutting through the rhetoric of such works as *The Romance of the Rose*, it tears off the labels with which women had been stiffened and stifled all through the Dark Ages, and sanctions what they had always been doing anyway – or allows them to do it well. You can find in the Bible what you will, to prove any point you like: I might pick out Deborah the wise, the Israelite Judge and prophetess, keeper of the tabernacle lamps and counsellor of men,[9] and Lydia, St Paul's first European convert to Christianity[10] and a successful merchant in the Middle East, trading in rich dyes distilled from purple mollusc shells by the Phoenicians. Both were real women renowned not for wickedness, but for using the talents God gave them.

Why this relaxation in the circumscription and definition of women should have happened now is a rather large question. It could pragmatically be ascribed to the demography of Europe during the first few centuries of the second millennium, the implication being that now women *had* to be taken seriously: there were too many – certainly in the upper classes – to ignore. I suspect it has more to do with intellectual enlightenment, with the wider scope, dissemination and discussion of theological and philosophical teachings signalled by the Renaissance, and an increase in education both for men (in schools and secular universities as well as in monasteries and other religious foundations before the dissolution) and for women (at home, at the odd German or Italian university and in nunneries). Not only was the Bible more accessible – at least to the clergy and certain heads of household, who would read from it each day – but the first works of biography of real women were also beginning to emerge now.

[25]

At first, it was vicarious biography: the story of Hildegard of Bingen (1098–1178) is reflected in her own reportage of celestial visions and glances off the texts she wrote herself.[11] Although coyly referring to herself as a *paupercula feminea forma*, a poor little womanly thing, Hildegard was a polymath: a mystic, preacher, papally endorsed prophet, botanist, physician, musician, playwright, and – to her the most important – interpreter of the word, and will, of God. Accounts of her visions were circulated amongst the crowds who heard her preach on her travels around Germany, and they were sensationally popular. Intellectuals read and inwardly digested her books on the theory of nature, and the nature of man; and doctors considered, no doubt with some bewilderment, her utterly unorthodox opinions on human sexuality:

> A man's love . . . is a blazing heat, like a fire on a blazing mountain, which can hardly be quenched, while [a woman's] is more like a wood-fire that is easy to quench: but a woman's love, in comparison with a man's, is like a sweet warmth coming from the sun, which brings forth fruits . . . When a woman is making love with a man, a sense of heat in her brain, which brings with it sensual delight, communicates the taste of that delight during the act and summons forth the emission of the man's seed. And when the seed has fallen into its place, that vehement heat from her brain draws the seed to itself and holds it . . . in the same way as a strong man can hold something enclosed in his fist.[12]

Giovanni Boccacio (who described female sexuality rather differently as the preternaturally voracious appetite of 'an imperfect creature excited by a thousand foul passions')[13] was one of the first to present a biographical collection of non-religious women: in *De Claris Mulieribus* (*Concerning Famous Women*) written between 1355 and 1359, he celebrated history's most notable pagan ladies, including, incidentally, Pope Joan. He did not feel the need to limit himself too strictly to accuracy, but it was the first step on the road to bigger and better things.

Important, too, in creating a kinder atmosphere for enterprising women, was the shift in Western Europe towards a feudal society. The Normans brought feudalism to England in 1066, along with an economic structure which elevated certain ladies (but naturally only the well-favoured middle and upper classes) and gave them specific custodial and financial duties. They started to manage estates, and to collect and dispose of income. Margaret Paston (1423–84) was one: being both the daughter and wife of wealthy and comparatively learned Norfolk landowners, she had a good education, a stout reputation, and sometimes almost overwhelming responsibilities to her name. Quite by chance, a copious collection of her letters to members of the Paston family survives, describing a life not that far removed from the one expected of the lady 'above rubies' in the passage from Proverbs. Margaret was frequently left in charge of the estate's land, tenants and administration when her husband John was on business in London, and her regular letters to him show how thorough a steward she was. When the demesne was threatened by boundary disputes (increasingly acrimonious in the Pastons' case) or caught up in the local power struggles of the Wars of the Roses, Margaret's duties grew decidedly dangerous:

> Right worshipful husband, I recommend myself to you . . .
> I was at Hellesdon on Thursday last and saw your place there, and in good faith, no-one could imagine how foul and horrible it appears unless they saw it for themselves. Many people come daily to wonder at it, from Norwich and other places, and they say what a shame it is . . . They [the opposing duke and his henchmen] made your tenants of Hellesdon and Drayton, with others, help break down the walls of both the place and the lodge – God knows evilly against their wills, but they dare not disobey for fear . . .[14]

[27]

> I . . . pray you to get some crossbows . . . and quarrel
> [crossbow bolts], for your houses here are so broken down
> that no-one can use a long-bow safely, though we had never
> so much need . . . And also I wish you would get two or
> three short poleaxes to keep inside, and as many armoured
> jackets as you may.

Nothing seems to faze Margaret too much, however: in almost
the next sentence of the same letter she is asking for

> . . . one pound of almonds and one pound of sugar, and . . .
> some woollen cloth to make your children's gowns from.
> You shall have the best price and choice from Hay's wife,
> so I am told. And . . . buy a yard of black broadcloth for
> a hood for me . . .[15]

At times, Margaret Paston's letters read more like a businesswoman's diary than a housewife's. But unlike the letters of
businessmen, hers bring in domestic details that illuminate her
life and reflect on her character. 'I pray you that you will wear
the ring with the image of St Margaret that I sent you till you come
home,' she wrote while heavily pregnant. 'You have left me such
a rememberance that makes me to think upon you both day and
night when I would sleep . . .' And she despairs of their daughter,
who grows up wayward and disobedient, eventually eloping with
the family bailiff: 'Remember you, and so do I, that we have lost
of her but a whore . . .' One can identify with Margaret, or at
least empathize with her, as with few of the women we have
met so far.

Margaret Paston was not self-employed, I suppose, in that
although she worked for a living, she did not choose how to do
it, nor was the money she earned her own to spend as she liked.
She fulfilled society's, and her family's, expectations in her working
life, just as the farmer's wife did, or the wife of a tradesman or

merchant. But she was frequently challenged, and rose to the challenge: she was a woman of considerable achievement, like other medieval gentlewomen who tended to come into their own once their husbands were away at court, at the Crusades, or on the battlefield. Many members of the ever-increasing mercantile class did the same when widowed. In fact, to many, widowhood proved the only gateway to independence and success.

It is a great boon to have objective documentary evidence of women's lives during the thirteenth and fourteenth centuries. Wills – both men's and women's – provide details of property and ownership; apprentices' indentures refer to female 'masters' and apprentices as well as male; books of household accounts mention particular tradeswomen, while Guild records list honourable widows managing their own workshops and occasionally operating as legally autonomous 'femmes soles'.[16] Often, the occupations in which these women were engaged are unsurprising, given tradition. As far back as Charlemagne's time, in the eighth century, highly organized workshops for women textile workers were encouraged as an important part of the economy of the Frankish Empire.[17] Anything to do with the wool and silk industries and with household activities was considered suitable work for a woman, hence the preponderance of spinsters, weavers, girdle-makers, brewers, bakers, inn and lodging-house keepers, regraters (market-traders) and so on. Wives' wages were generally lower than their husbands', because it was assumed that wives already had a roof over their heads; widows, on the other hand, could be virtually self-employed. And whereas men were bound by an Act of Parliament (1363) to limit themselves to a single trade, women were allowed to change and to diversify. Teenage girls would be lodged with friends or relations, should circumstances allow, to help out with their family business and save some money towards a dowry, but specific training might be thought risky when one did not know the trade or business of one's future husband. When a woman married, she saved her husband having to pay wages to someone else and, if practicable, augmented the family finances with some little domestic sideline.

That is the stuff of standard social history. At the same time it is against this essentially home-based background that certain women stand in sharp relief.

The first is someone mentioned frustratingly *en passant* in the account books of the court of King Henry III (1216–72) as Mariot de Ferars:[18] she had been paid the considerable sum of £75 for providing the King with horses, saddles and harness. Someone else acting by royal appointment was Marie Valence,[19] who broke the monopoly of traders supplying passing crusaders in Marseilles in 1248 by craftily establishing her butcher's business on an island just offshore. Half a century later the wheelwright Dyonisia la Roura[20] was awarded a lucrative contract to furnish all the vehicles needed to transport a royal party's visit to Scotland.

One of the most enterprising women was Juliana of Ely, who flourished (and I use the word advisedly) around 1325. Juliana was an entrepreneur. She held the enviable post of head-gardener at the Bishop of Ely's manor in Cambridgeshire. There she coaxed an array of fruit and vegetables from the fens: peas, beans and leeks for consumption at the Manor House, and apples, pears, cherries, nuts and plums for sale by the household's steward, or 'in the courtyard' at a stall. No doubt she made a profit. She also leased fishponds and meadowland; she is noted in The Court Rolls[21] for being involved in various illicit land deals, and is said to have kept the local 'villeins' occupied by organizing a working-party for a few days each year to dig in the garden – a ready source of free labour. She must have been both strong and peremptory; not a woman, I should imagine, to be trifled with.

By the fifteenth century, women were not only managing existing enterprises, but establishing their own. Unfortunately, for many of them we only have their names: Denise the Bookbinder,[22] or Anastasia the Illuminator,[23] or the bell-founders Johanna Hill (died

1441) and Johanna Sturdy (died c.1460),[24] whose foundry was in Aldgate, London, and some of whose bells still ring today. Others have made more impact on documentary history.

Joan Buckland,[25] by the time she died in 1462, was an exceedingly wealthy woman. She was the daughter of a moderately successful fishmonger in London, the wife of a markedly successful fishmonger, again in London, and during the twenty-six years of her widowhood the head of a spectacularly successful shipping company, licensed to victual the fleets of Kings Henry V and VI in Calais. Alice Chester (died 1485)[26] was in the same sort of business. Her husband, a Somerset shipowner, died in 1470, and Alice spent the fifteen years until her own death in expanding the business into one of the foremost import/export operations in Bristol. She brought in iron from Spain, trading it for cloth, which she also sold to Lisbon and Flanders; so rich did she and her son John become in the process that she decided to invest in the erection of a dockside crane, 'for the saving of merchants' goods of the town and of strangers.' She spent money on All Saints' Church in Bristol as well, making sure she would be remembered not only as a prosperous woman, but a pious one too.

Good women were not often celebrated publicly in the fifteenth century. Not ordinary good women, anyway. Those stereotypical ones, like the saints and queens who found themselves shunted about in the previous chapter, still functioned as symbols of moral purity and, with the rise of the art of chivalry, embodied in *The Romance of the Rose*, there appeared an array of fabulously virtuous creatures to inspire men to courtly love and heavenly delight. This was a highly structured age as far as culture and the arts were concerned, but not exclusively so. Someone gave me a diary a few years ago, illustrated with facsimile illuminations of medieval women working.[27] It was captivating: gone were all those familiar ladies looking slightly fey and invariably dressed in gowns of cerulean blue, and in their place were *real women*. Instead of suckling adult-looking Jesuses, or gazing soulfully at angels, or offering their long white hands to smirking suitors, they were designing frescoes, building walls, working in jewellery shops, as apothecaries' assistants, as sculptors; there is a blacksmith (looking slightly nonplussed, it must be said), several artists, musicians playing dulcimers, viols, harps, or even bagpipes, and perhaps my favourite of all, a cook sitting by a fire, absentmindedly stirring a stewpot while engrossed in the book on her lap.

They are so refreshing, images like these. While well aware that illuminators were professional illustrators, and as capable of raising a laugh with ridiculous scenarios as they were of recording social history, I still maintain that their work is a valuable source for anyone curious enough to look beyond the literary formulae of the time and see what wives and daughters really did.

It is impossible to know which of these exuberant little vignettes portray particular women, except in the case of Christine de Pizan, that is: she appears again and again, sometimes painted by Anastasia, the female illuminator mentioned earlier, often sitting at a desk and writing or reading, clad almost invariably in a dark blue dress with white piping at the hem and sleeves, wearing a neat, white, crescent-shaped head-dress, and occasionally with an amiable-looking dog at her heels.

Christine de Pizan (*c.*1364–*c.*1430) is one of my favourite heroines. Not only was she the first professional woman writer of all (working because she had a family to support), but the books she wrote were about women – about their nature, their history, their influence and, most radical of all, their rights. What is more, she somehow managed, in a man's world, to be both popular and well-respected. She is the perfect antidote to the over-excesses of Aristotle, Bishop Marbod, Jean de Meun and Aquinas.

Christine had an auspicious upbringing. She was born in Venice, although soon moved to Paris where her father, Tommaso da Pizzano, was installed as counsellor and court astrologer to Charles V. There she was educated (much against the advice of her mother, who wished a happy, not a learned life for her daughter). She paid tribute to her father's insistence in indulging her passion for collecting the 'precious stones' of knowledge in her greatest work, *Le Livre de la Cité des Dames* (*The Book of the City of Ladies*, 1405), where she describes herself listening to the allegorical voice of 'Rectitude':

> ... [i]t is not all men, especially not the most intelligent, who agree with the view that it is a bad idea to educate women. However, it's true that those who are not very clever come out with this opinion because they don't want women to know more than they do. Your own father, who was a great astrologer and philosopher, did not believe that knowledge of the sciences reduced a woman's worth ... It's obvious to me that you do not esteem yourself any less for having this knowledge: in fact, you seem to treasure it, and quite rightly so.[28]

At the age of fifteen, Christine married Etienne de Castel, a court secretary with whom she subsequently had three children; that same year, however, Charles V died, and in the subsequent political upheaval both father and husband fell heavily out of favour. Tommaso died in 1385, and Etienne four years later, leaving Christine in charge of her mother, her children and a niece with whom they lived.

Christine was also left a complex financial problem: when her husband expired of fever while away on business, he was owed substantial amounts of money, which his widow would have to recover for her living. To compound her difficulties, she was still waiting for the payment of her father's pension, and for permission to access her own inheritance. She describes subsequent legal battles (of Dickensian ramifications) with weary incredulity, remembering how many times she spent whole mornings at the Palais de Justice in winter, dying of cold, unable to discover the precise state of Etienne's finances. It was the custom for married men not to reveal their business affairs completely to their wives, which Christine considered nonsensical. Many women were, like her, 'not flippant but wise', and well able to cope with the management of money.[29]

It took six years to recover part, at least, of what was owed. Meanwhile, Christine had to be 'six people at once' to find the family enough to live on: 'It became clear to me that I should have to start working.' Although she is not specific, it is thought that for the first year or two Christine worked amongst several women scribes and copyists known to be active in Paris at the time, learning as she went along, and thus equipping herself for the career that was to follow.

In 1399 the first of Christine's original writings was published (i.e. copied and distributed). She wrote ballads and lyric poetry, establishing herself as a deft and delicate wordsmith very much after the fashion of the day. But as her success grew amongst the aristocratic circles in which she still moved, so her work became more significant. And while her technique might not be new – she used the literary devices of her predecessors and peers – her subject matter, emphatically, was.

In *Le Livre de la Mutation de la Fortune* (1403: a vast work of 23,636 lines) she used her own family's dramatic change in fortune to illustrate just how fickle fate can be, and what might be done about it. For women, the message is stark: to succed in the world of men, women must become men themselves. They must change their weak natures (or what is perceived to be weakness) and, like Christine, assume 'masculine' strengths. [30]

She was certainly treated as male when commissioned to write the authorized biography of her family's erstwhile patron, Charles V, by his brother in 1404; and an editor of a military manual she produced much later thought that for credibility's sake he had better suggest it had been written by a man, since no one was going to believe such expertise possible in a female – even if that female were Christine de Pizan. But it was a foolish notion – as

Christine's words at the head of this chapter recognize – to hide her sex: she quickly came to realize that only as a woman could she express, through her work, what she needed to.

The City of Ladies is Christine's best-known work. It is a huge construction, an allegorical citadel built, she says, by strength of mind rather than body, on ground cleared of basketfuls of dust (i.e. the received wisdom of the past) and the rubble of men's misconceptions of women, and mortared together with ink and dignity. Its architects are three ladies who come to Christine in a vision: Reason, Recitude and Justice. Together, the four discuss why this city should be founded, why it has never been founded before, and why, once built, it will stand strong and protective of women's reputation for ever.

The inspiration for *The City of Ladies* was Christine's instinctive reaction to reading much of the contemporary writing I have quoted in this chapter (and the last) about the inherent immorality, impotence and incompetence of women. Specifically, she cites *The Romance of the Rose*: she had already responded robustly in the 'Querelle', writing letters and essays in refutation of Jean de Meun's diseased concept of femininity. 'No matter which way I looked at it,' she says, 'and no matter how much I turned the question over in my mind, I could find no evidence from my own experience [and learning] to bear out such a negative view of female nature . . .'[31] Taking as evidence Boccacio's *De Claris Mulieribus*, she goes on to prove her point, listing history's good women, including the Amazons and Artemisia. She counters the arguments of 'philosophers, poets, and orators too numerous to mention, who all seem to speak with one voice and are unanimous in their view that female nature is wholly given up to vice'[32] by describing how women *feel*: what a mother's love feels like, what injustice feels like, what it feels like to speak sensibly while no one listens, and to act thoughtfully while no one notices.

The final section of the book is like a rallying-cry: addressing herself to all women 'whether of high, middle, or low social rank', she urges them to be on their guard, and stand firm in their city of good sense.

> My ladies, see how these men assail you on all sides, and accuse you of every vice imaginable. Prove them all wrong by showing how principled you are . . . Act in such a way that you can say, like the Psalmist, 'The evil done by the wicked will fall on their own heads.'[33]

Christine knew her audience. She knew that literary fashion embraced artifice, and enjoyed a robust argument. She also had confidence in her ability to write well: she was just daring enough in *The City of Ladies* to provoke, without losing credibility. It was a critical success. So was its sequel, *Le Livre des Trois Vertus* (*The Book of Three Virtues*, also 1405), a sort of moral etiquette book for women – 'of all estates'. She was never over-strident in defence of her sex: she once wrote that she would like to be remembered not as a champion but as a diligent daughter of God (made, she was careful to say, in His image). She wrote in *Le Livre de la Mutation de la Mutation de la Fortune* that the one ambition she had cherished throughout her career was to engender the sympathy and prayers of her readers and listeners. If they should say one Pater Noster for the repose of her soul, she would be amply rewarded. [34]

It is ironic that few women outside court circles would have been able to read Christine's work, and hard to tell how much impact it had on those who could. Now, however, for her life as well as her work, she is remembered as the first person to credit her gender with God-given dignity.

When William Caxton went into business as Britain's first printer, one of the earliest books he chose to publish, in 1490, was a translation into English of Christine's military manual, *Le Livre des Faits d'Armes et de Chivalrie*. A Norfolk housewife

called Margery Kempe followed hot on her heels, with the publisher Wynkyn de Worde bringing out extracts of her rather racy
autobiography in 1501.[35] Margery, though, did not write for a
living. She wrote because she had promised God to let people know
what a wicked woman she had once been and what a splendid one
– through atonement and pilgrimage – she eventually became. Her
descriptions of her earlier self are irresistible, strutting about King's
Lynn with 'gold pipes on her head, and her hoods and tippets . . .
slashed and underlaid with various colours between the slashes,
so that she would be all the more stared at, and all the more
esteemed.' She went into business at one stage as a brewer 'out
of sheer covetousness . . . and was one of the greatest brewers in
the town . . . for three or four years until she lost a great deal of
money' (and the ale inexplicably kept going flat). Next she tried
flour-milling, but the horses she had bought to turn the millstones
refused to work.

> Then it was noised about the town that neither man nor
> beast would serve the said creature . . . Then she asked God
> for mercy, and forsook her pride, her covetousness, and the
> desire that she had for worldly dignity, and did great bodily
> penance, and began to enter the way of everlasting life as
> shall be told hereafter.[36]

Perhaps Margery was not confident enough to succeed as an
author? (She dictated her life-story to a monk, because she could
not actually write herself.) She falls back, having failed in two of
her chosen careers, on confession that ambition is really sinful
pride, and that courting success in the temporal world means
spurning the spiritual. It must have sapped so many spirited
women's confidence, that no one expected them to sustain
themselves, either physically and morally, on their own. And
worse than that: they were literally damned if they tried.

But yet again, we are forced to consider how relevant to real working women all these rather remote edicts actually were. While Christine was undoubtedly successful, and those business-women like Joan Buckland and Alice Chester thrived, for all we know Europe was bustling with women dentists, clock-makers, stone-masons, scaffolders, and goodness knows what else. I have come across several printers of the fourteenth century, including Margaretha Prüss (*c.*1550s),[37] operating in Strasbourg, and Jane Yetswiert (born 1541),[38] who held a Crown patent to print all English Common Law books from 1595–8. (Both were widows – Margaretha prodigiously so, having wed and buried three husbands in succession.) There was at least one woman money-lender in thirteenth-century Paris (the Jewess Bona, of Dog Lane);[39] several master goldsmiths (including German Drutgin von Caster, specially appointed artisan to the Holy Roman Emperor),[40] and an English expert in 'hawking, hunting, fishing, and armorie',[41] who wrote a book about her sporting pursuits in 1481.

One of my favourite illuminated manuscripts of this period shows a lady, dressed in crimson and gold, decorously prodding away at a quarry wall with a hammer. At every touch, cascades of jewels are tumbling down to her feet. She has a shovel ready to scoop them up and load them into a basket already groaning with treasure. In the same way, like Christine de Pizan, once you start to clear away the mould of received wisdom and ignorance (often the same thing), all sorts of gems start glinting out at you.

In fact, I think that particular illustration was meant as an allegory for the pursuit of knowledge (which makes me admire it none the less): the lady miner is showing how rich and ennobling a business the search for truth and wisdom can be. Learning yields treasure to all who take the time and make the effort to seek it.

Foreshadowing the great educational debate of the seventeenth century there are several figures in the medieval age who wrote bravely about the need for women to be allowed, if they wish and are capable, to study. One of these was the Italian Laura de Cereta (1469–99), whose unnatural ambition was to become a professional author like her countrywoman Christine. Her personal circumstances were not as urgent as Christine's: although left a widow when her merchant husband died in about 1485, Laura was childless. She had a father, who was supportive both financially and intellectually, and encouraged the publication of her first volume of letters in 1488,[42] but when he died as well, Laura lacked the confidence to carry on with her writing. She lacked the literary finesse, too: her work was considered too overpowering, too unleavened, to be profitably palatable:

> ... [S]ome women worry about the styling of their hair, the elegance of their clothes, and the pearls and other jewellery they wear on their fingers. Others love to say cute little things, to hide their feelings behind a mask of tranquillity, to indulge in dancing, and to lead pet dogs around on a leash . . . But those women for whom the quest for the good [i.e. knowledge] represents a higher value restrain their young spirits and ponder better plans. They harden their bodies with sobriety and toil, they control their tongues, they carefully monitor what they hear, they ready their minds for all-night vigils, and they rouse their minds for the contemplation of probity . . . For knowledge is not given as a gift but by study. For a mind free, keen, and unyielding . . . grows in the depth and breadth.[43]

Gentler exhortations to women at the end of the medieval period to cultivate a little independence (within reason) came in the form of the various instruction manuals popular at the time, like de Pizan's *Le Livre des Trois Vertus*, dedicated to princesses, ladies at court, women of rank, artisans, chambermaids, prostitutes, labourers' wives – even 'poor people'. The gist of this book is that all women should be aware of their financial circumstances, of their husband's duties (so that they may take over if necessary) and of their unique qualities as managers and peace-makers. Another good example is *How the Good Wife Taught her Daughter* (anon., *c*.1430), with its salutary advice to love God, and always to go to church (without letting the rain stop you, without wiggling your shoulders on the way, or gossiping when you get there). Don't be seen over-eating or drunk, it warns, or at wrestling-matches and cock-fights. Otherwise you will be regarded as (most heinous of fates) 'a strumpet or a gigggelot [sic]'. Above all, says the Good Wife, be cheerful and true to yourself, as well as to God and your husband.

A somewhat more challenging book of the same genre is Thomas Tusser's alarming *Five Hundred Points of Good Husbandry* (1580), which includes the gloomy couplet: 'Some respite to husbands the weather may send, but huswives' affairs have never an end.' And there are others, some aimed only at moral probity, but most concerned with practical efficiency and domestic harmony as well. It is in volumes such as these that the traditional ideals of womanhood finally came down to earth. The focus shifted from myths and symbols of impossible virtue, through stories of celebrated heroines of the past, to (more or less) sensible guidance for the ordinary, modern female. You could be a good woman, these books suggest, and you could be a useful woman – not only to others, but to yourself. You could determine the course of your life by *doing* things, and be judged by what you do rather than by what you are.

At last women had permission to function as intelligent members of humanity! After all the pontification of the Dark and Middle Ages, the future of the self-sufficient woman seemed set fair. Except what people – even historians – often fail to realize is that welcome as it might have been in many ways, women did not *need* permission to live as they wished. They simply needed the right circumstances and the right spirit. All the busy, confident women we've discussed so far would (with one or two exceptions) not have cared a fig for any rules of conduct: they had their own integrity, and relied on that for their success.

Nor would some of them have cared much for a good reputation, either. These are the women I have kept until last in this chapter of medieval accomplishment: the anti-heroines of the Renaissance age, whom some would consider poor advertisements for the independence of working women, but who should really be relished as real adventuresses.

Think of a typical medieval scene: there might be a prettily turreted castle, for example, a garden growing around it, studded with neat little roses and apple trees, a beautiful maiden will be strolling along in a high-bodiced gown (the sleeves slashed like Margery Kempe's) and a tall pointy hat with a veil. Kneeling down amongst the daisies at her feet will be a comely young man, dressed in tunic and tights, with a lute and a longing gaze. He's that most romantic of figures, the troubadour.

Troubadours were professional poets and singer-songwriters, travelling sometimes with other performers but often operating alone, whose lyrics (traditionally in the Provençal language) celebrated love – rather like *The Romance of the Rose* but less high-falutin', and with tunes. And, rather surprisingly, there were women troubadours as well as men. Some doubled as camp followers, accompanying the men of the Crusades, or other motley bands of travellers, fighters or artists, and were responsible for setting and clearing up camps, digging defensive trenches and cleaning weapons, as well as the usual domestic duties. Others were solely entertainers. The Countess of Dia was one of twenty such soloists known to have worked in France during the twelfth century, and her lyrics are refreshingly earthy:

> Fair friend, charming and good,
>   When shall I hold you in my power?
> And lie beside you for an hour,

[41]

And amorous kisses give to you;
Know that I would give almost anything
To have you in my husband's place,
But only if you swear
To do everything I desire . . .[44]

The 'Countess' reminds me of an earlier incarnation of Chaucer's Wife of Bath: sexy, confident and robust.

There were more amorphous bands of vagabond women, apparently, roaming the countryside at the same time as the troubadours, but this time terrorizing rather than diverting the locals. I should like to know a lot more of the blood-curdling Irishwoman Geraldine Desmond,[45] said to have 'killed all who opposed her and [taken] possession of their property,' or of the 800-strong gang of females who decended on Frankfurt in 1391, paralysing the city and virtually holding it to ransom.[46]

Thanks to court records, it is possible to glimpse one or two characters a little more clearly. Alipo the forger, for example, who was arraigned in Paris in 1390 for issuing counterfeit coins (and, incidentally, for infanticide),[47] or Jacoba the physician, again in Paris, who was charged in 1322 with ministering to the sick, and diagnosing their illnesses, without proper qualifications.[48] One medieval malefactor we do know a suspicious amount about is Dame Alice Kyteler, who became the richest woman in the land through serially marrying – and disposing of – a choice selection of Ireland's most solvent sons. She was called a witch, although she never burned for it: I see her rather as an astute operator, and possessed of a particularly loyal and influential circle of friends.

Alice enjoyed a head start in her avaricious career, being born of sound and wealthy Kilkenny stock, and although she was considered a haughty woman, this seemed to be justified. She married a banker and money-lender called William Outlawe, and they had a son, Roger, whom Alice worshipped. William died, however, sometime around 1302. Adam le Blund was her next husband,

and lasted until 1311; he was followed by Richard de Valle, and finally Sir John le Poer, who in 1324, like his predecessors, became gravely ill with alarming symptoms of a general malaise, punctuated by the falling out of hair and fingernails.

Alice's various stepchildren were cynical, and they were not alone: her house was searched, and loot, including unmistakable phials of poison and instruments of satanic worship, were sent to the local bishop, who promptly excommunicated her. She was also arrested, with her son Roger and maid Petronilla de Meath, on charges including the pernicious preparation of potions made from 'the hair of criminals who had been hanged, nails from dead men's fingers [plenty of those about the house] . . . and flesh of babies who had died unbaptized.'[49] Petronilla was the first woman in Ireland to be burned for witchcraft, on 3 November 1324; Roger and his mother escaped, however, and helped by 'aristocratic' friends they fled to England, where Alice lived comfortably and died, most probably, in her bed.

The more wicked these women become, the less one seems to be able to rely on historical accuracy. They are certainly shady characters, but rooted in fact, I feel sure. However when it comes to Mother Shipton, I have my doubts, just as I have occasional doubts about Pope Joan. What is important, though, is that like Alice Kyteler, Mother Shipton was a woman celebrated in her own time, and not a later fictitious invention.

This is the authorized version of Ursula Shipton's life and career.[50] She was born Ursula Sontheil in 1488 in Knaresborough, North Yorkshire. Her mother Agatha was an unmarried orphan, taken to court on charges of immorality when it was discovered she was pregnant with Ursula. The case was dismissed after Agatha quietly pointed out to the judge that to her certain knowledge at least two of the women present in court (as spectators) were themselves with child *by him*. Ursula was duly born, in a cave down by the River Nidd, but soon afterwards Agatha evaporated from the story and the baby was left to the care of the parish nurse.

Ursula was not a bonny baby: her nose was her crowning glory, 'being of unproportionable length, with many crooks and turnings, adorned with great pimples . . . which, like vapours of brimstone, gave strong lustre in the night' – so strong that the nurse 'needed no other candle to dress herself except the babe's nose.'[51]

We don't know much of Ursula's girlhood, but there is an impression that it was passed in domestic chaos, with furniture habitually whirling itself about the air around her, or disappearing up the chimney. Even Ursula herself was once found firmly wedged well above the fireplace in her cot. But neither she nor the nurse seems to have been unduly disquieted: 'be contented,' Ursula would say, 'there is nothing here that will hurt . . .' At twenty-four, Ursula married a brave local lad called Toby Shipton, a carpenter, and together they settled into comparatively comfortable respectability, with their own house, a servant or two, and Ursula's sooth-saying business. Mother Shipton had a knack for knowing things: she knew where long-lost objects were to be found, or who was to be blamed for local crimes and misdemeanours; most profitably of all, she could predict the future. She became an oracle, predicting royal births and deaths, foreseeing the Armada and the Fire of London (even Samuel Pepys credited her with that), and – most marvellous of all to those who knew about it – the circumstances of Cardinal Wolsey's death in 1530. He was on his way to his palace at York, but only got as far as Cawood Castle, within sight of the Minster, before Henry VIII sent for him to return, for trial, to London. He never arrived, perishing of 'a violent looseness' at Leicester on the way.

Ursula predicted it all in great detail, writing: the Cardinal shall see York, but not reach it, and he'll die within days of the journey. Wolsey's death made Ursula's name, and to this day her wondrous prophecies have been printed and sold to an amazed and admiring public.[52] She died in 1561, on a day and at a time she naturally knew, and broadcast, in advance. The cave where she was born, next to a grotto of 'miraculous' petrifying waters called

'Mother Shipton's Well', has become a shrine to her perspicacity and business acumen, shifting pamphlets and souvenirs by the thousand every year. She's even got her own website now. And it still sends a shiver down my spine when I read one series of her prophecies (uttered in the middle of the sixteenth century, but obviously rendered into doggerel a little later):

> Carriages without horses shall go
>   And accidents fill the world with woe;
> Around the world thoughts shall fly
>   In the twinkling of an eye;
> The world upside down shall be,
>   And gold be found at the root of a tree.
> Through hills man shall ride,
>   And no horse be at his side.
> Under water men shall walk,
>   Shall ride, shall sleep, shall talk . . .
> Iron in the water shall float,
>   As easily as a wooden boat.
> Gold shall be found and shown
>   In a land that's not yet known . . .
> The world to an end shall come,
>   In eighteen hundred and eighty-one.[53]

It's a pity about the last line, but why let facts get in the way of a good story?

That is a problem with this whole tale, of course: it is obviously as heavily embroidered a biography as one can get. And however likely it is, there is no *proof* Ursula Shipton was ever paid a penny for her predictions. But the point I find significant about her is her obvious benignity. Ugly as she was, and weird as her powers were perceived to be, she was called 'Mother' Shipton. She proves that it was possible to be an eccentric woman in late medieval England without being labelled a witch. She was a performer, and rarely is her life and work referred to without some degree of the respect and affection she must have evoked while alive (except in the case of a few rather apoplectic Victorian commentators).

A lot of women worked hard, in their various ways, for that right to be eccentric – perhaps no one harder than Christine de Pizan. How long their legacy lasted, however, as the Middle Ages drew to a close and the harsher light of the Age of Reason dawned, we shall see.

3

MADDE PRANCKES AND
MERRY MOLLS

I please myself, and care not else who loves me.

'Moll Cutpurse'[1]

MUCH HAPPENED BETWEEN THE DEATH of Ursula Shipton in 1561 (three years after the accession of Elizabeth I) and, say, the French Revolution of 1789, to heighten the profile of ordinary women in European society. By 'ordinary' I mean non-noblewomen, and probably even uneducated ones. The image of Elizabeth herself, commanding and dazzling fair Albion from 1558–1603, was not exactly unhelpful. Oriana, the self-styled Virgin Queen, flower of the English Renaissance and yet entirely her own woman, may have appeared a near-mythical figure to most of her subjects, but her political acumen and phenomenal stamina proved unequivocally that mortal females (albeit queens) *on their own* could be ruthless, wise and, above all, unassailably powerful.

There had been powerful queens before, of course: the freakish Boudicca, who is said by Tacitus to have led her people, the Iceni of modern East Anglia, against the Romans in the first century AD, leaving Colchester, London and St Albans burning in her wake and 70,000 Romans dead. Or the gentler Queen Philippa (c.1314–69), wife of Edward III, credited with introducing the woollen industry to Norwich, and establishing 'factories' where women worked comfortably and respectably 'inventing English clothes'.[2] But no queen before was as independent, influential and famous as Elizabeth.

Part of Elizabeth's legacy was a burgeoning merchant class in Britain (in which businesswomen flourished not only as widows, as Mistresses Buckland and Chester had done in medieval times, but also as wives and even spinsters); from the late sixteenth century onwards trade boundaries extended wider and wider, with the growth of foreign adventurism (or colonialism) and opportunities in America and India for enterprising families.

Meanwhile, at home, the Civil Wars of 1642–9 mustered extremes of loyalty and resourcefulness from women, and bravery of shocking ferocity. As in all wars, the normal rules of society were suspended, and women were allowed to behave – as Margaret Paston had had to – 'beyond their sex'. So heroines began to emerge like the 'Gallant She-Souldier' celebrated in a ballad of the time:

> Her Husband was a Souldier, and to the wars did go,
> And she would be his Comrade, the truth of all is so.
> She put on Man's Apparel, and bore him company,
> As many in the Army for truth can testify.[3]

These heroines were usually depicted as impatient wives or venturesome whores who counterfeited their sex and fought for Puritan or Roundhead alike. There are countless stories of courage and cunning involving all sorts of combatants: from Yorkshire cavalryman Jane Ingleby, wounded at Marston Moor,[4] to the Portsmouth 'intelligencer', or spy, alias 'the poor woman', who smuggled messages from Charles I to his Queen in 1642.[5]

One of my favourites is Elizabeth Alkin, nicknamed 'Parliament

Joan', who set up a hospital for wounded rebels in London. She was paid £30 6s 8d for her service, but was as generous as she was compassionate, and used to disburse her own money amongst those in her care who had none. She went on to nurse in Harwich, before turning undercover as a spy and – eventually – a journalist for the Puritan cause.[6]

Mrs Alkin was lucky: she was not only paid for her work, but granted a house for life and some status as an active sponsor of, and participant in, the Commonwealth. Usually such 'masculine femininity' was only to be encouraged for the duration, and it is a feature of the Civil Wars, like the Indian Mutiny a century later and the two World Wars, that when life was supposed to ratchet back to normal after the conflict, and the old roles be assumed again, many women who had tasted and relished independence and unwonted proactivity, were simply not prepared to sink back into submission. This may well be why the dissenters and nonconformists of the later seventeenth century were so staunchly supported by 'well-affected' women.[7] The 'Friends of Truth', dubbed the Quakers in 1650 and founded by George Fox, deemed women entirely equal to men in spirit, intellect and capability. The Diggers and the Levellers and the Millenarians[8] – all sects which prospered during the Commonwealth – stood for the equality of mankind and despised social hierarchy, a premise which readily embraced the grievances of women. That their political discontent was recognized at all was a breakthrough, and soon women were beginning to debate their own status, prospects, even *rights*, with both conviction and result.

A landmark in the legal history of women's rights was reached as early as 1632 with the publication of *The Lawes Resolutions of Women's Rights: or, The Lawes Provision for Woemen* [sic]. It declared itself a 'Methodicall Collection of Such Statutes and Customes, with the Cases, Opinions, Arguments and points of Learning in the Law, as doe properly concerne Women'. Despite

[49]

its encouraging title, though, it makes rather glum reading, stating for posterity all that women cannot do:

> Women have no voyce in Parliament, they make no Lawes, they consent to none, they abrogate none. All of them are understood either married or to bee married and their desires subject to their husband . . .[9]

There is no remedy, regrets the author, before adding deliciously that for all that, it is obvious 'some women can shift it well enough'. These are the women this chapter will focus on. The debate on women's position in society, and what they did about it, will be discussed in Chapter 4, but for now, it is women who can 'shift it' who count – real eccentrics, in a turbulent age, who kicked up their heels and rebelled.

Before we get to the mavericks, I suppose it is important to know a little more of the gradually enlightening background against which they were operating. There were still various occupations deemed suitable for women during the late sixteenth, the seventeenth, and the early eighteenth centuries. Textiles still loomed large, of course; women were traditionally responsible for the mechanics of the silk industry (doing everything from collecting and emptying the cocoons, to drawing the threads through the loom, to designing pattern and texture – although strangely, rarely pulling the loom themselves); in Flanders they picked at intricate lacework until their eyes blurred; in England, where a division between those who produced goods and those who sold them was just beginning to develop, some created the rich embroideries and crewel-work that made their craft famous, while others more prosaically sewed shrouds, made girdles and stuffed mattresses; in the provinces they carded wool and spun it. But in London, when times were hard and no one was buying silk (mending what they had instead) the seamstresses started to diversify:

When the looms of the Spitalfields silk workers were still
and the industry was in slump the reelers made fireworks
at home or sewed condoms for a Mrs Phelps [or Philips]
who had the equivalent of a mail order firm throughout
Europe . . .[10]

Now there was a woman with vision . . . In an advertisement
issued at her premises at 'the sign of the Golden Fan and
Rising Sun' in Orange Court (near present-day Leicester Square)
Mrs Phelps claimed thirty-five years' experience in making
Colonel Cundum's 'implements of safety',[11] thoughtfully sewn
from silk rather than the customary sheep gut. These 'fine
machines' were offered for purchase in bulk, with the particular assurance that 'Ambassadors, Foreigners, Gentlemen and
Captains of Ships, may be supplied with any quantity' they
required.

Mrs Phelps used also to sell medical supplies, especially 'skins
and bladders for apothecaries, chymists, and druggists', as well
as 'all sorts of perfumes'. She was on the fringes of a particularly robust group of women, whose enterprising careers
flourished during the early years of the eighteenth century: the
quacks.

Women and nursing wove together almost as neatly as women
and textiles. It had always been part of a female's domestic
duty to care for the ill. Nuns traditionally tended infirmaries for
the sick, and properly educated ladies, like Christine de Pizan,
would be expected to reset the dislocated limbs of their menfolk injured while jousting, perhaps, or hunting, or fighting for
their honour.[12] However, midwifery was the only branch of
medicine in which formally uneducated women were allowed
to pursue a career, or even to charge for their services – until
now.

Quackery – so called for the way the more crass of its
practitioners called out to advertise themselves – was a rich

business. In an age of smallpox, where cosmetic artifice meant so much, booths and back-street bazaars sprang up all over England promising the world to its blemished people. A 'Gentlewoman' of St Martin's Lane offered a bewildering selection of treasures including:

> . . . a most incomparable Wash to beautifie the Face, agreeable to all . . . which takes off pimples, freckles, morphew [eruptions] or what else may obstruct a fair and lovely complexion . . . She hath also a most Delicate Pomatum, which is wonderfully agreeable to be used with it. A Summer's day is too short to demonstrate the full virtues of both these, therefore for brevity's sake she omits it . . . She hath a fine lip-salve . . . She hath most curious Masks and Forehead cloths, which take out all spots, pits, scars . . . and also all wrinkles of the face.[13]

Mrs Mary Green went one better, claiming not only to be able to cover up impurities and imperfections, but to banish them altogether:

> Mrs Atkins, a Midwife in Scroop's Court against St. Andrew's Church, Holbourn, [who] was lame in all her limbs, did for Five years consult the Ablest Doctors and likewise THE WHOLE COLLIDGE OF PHYSICIANS, was perfectly cured by Mary Green. She hath also cured Mrs Dixter in Hanging-Sword Alley in Fleet Street, and Mr. Vaughan . . . who was troubled with the Ptsick [psittacosis] and Mrs Batler . . . who had a White swelling [?] of which she was perfectly cured . . .[14]

Even more specialized was the widowed Lady Read, whose husband had (for a short time) been appointed 'sworn-oculist-

in-ordinary' to King George I. She professed herself an ophthal-
mologist, capable of curing people's blindness by 'couching' them:
literally flicking off their cataracts with a fingernail.[15]

We do not, of course, have any reliable testament to the successes
of such as Mrs Atkins and Lady Read (although couching was a
recognized – if rather short-term – treatment for cataracts). The
two arch-quacks of the period, though, were celebrated at the
very highest level: Sarah Mapp justifiably so, but definitely not
the outrageous Joanna Stephens.

Mrs Stephens (died 1774) was a publicist of consummate skill.
Working as a high class quack in London, she announced in 1736
that she had, at last, found the definitive cure for that scourge
of the modern age: 'calculus', or kidney stones. She added that
a number of persons of quality were willing to undersign her
claim, and so they did; there followed a two-year period of great
success, during which Mrs Stephens, becoming more and more
famous by the minute, charged noticeably higher fees than many
of the other medics in the market, and eventually published her
intention to sell her cure for the good of her country – and for
£5,000 (to be raised by subscription and lodged at Drummond's
Bank).[16]

So wildly inflated was this woman's reputation by now, whether
on solid grounds or not it's hard to tell, that a substantial list
of aristocratic ladies and gentlemen added their names to the
list of subscribers, among them the Earl of Godolphin (who
pledged £100) and the Bishop of Oxford (ten guineas), but all
they could raise between them was £1,356. This was hardly
enough for Joanna, and so, riskily, she applied to the government
to make up the sum. A Commission of Enquiry was duly appointed,
with the result that an Act of Parliament was passed expressly to
allow Mrs Stephens to be 'rewarded' from public funds for her
miraculous cure.

The *London Gazette* of 16 June 1739 was amongst the first to
publish the precious ingredients:

[53]

The medicines are a Powder, a Decoction [solution], and Pills.

The Powder consists of Egg-shells and Snails – both calcined [burned to dust].

The Decoction is made by boiling some herbs (together with a ball, which consists of soap, swine's cresses [a plant] burnt to blackness and honey) in water.

The Pills consist of Snails calcined, wild carrot seeds, burdock seeds, ashen keys, hips and hawes – all burnt to blackness – Alicant soap, and honey.

The method for mixing and administering the remedy seems impossibly abstruse:

Take Hen's Egg-Shells, well drained from the Whites, dry and clean, crush them small with the hands, and fill a Crucible of the twelfth Size (which contains nearly three Pints) with them lightly, place it in the Fire, and cover it with a Tile; then heap Coals over it that it may be in the midst of a very strong, clear Fire, till the Egg-Shells be calcin'd to a greyish-white, and acquire an acrid salt taste; this will take up eight Hours at least. After they are thus calcin'd put them into a dry, clean earthen Pan . . . Let the Pan stand uncovered in a dry Room for two Months, and no longer. In this time the Egg-Shells will become of a milder taste, and that part that is sufficiently calcin'd will fall into a Powder of such a Fineness as to pass through a common Hair-Sieve, which is to be done accordingly.

In like manner, take Garden Snails with their Shells, clean'd from the Dirt, fill a Crucible of the same Size with them whole, cover it, and place it in a Fire, as before, till the Snails have done Smoking . . . They are then to be taken out of the Crucible, and immediately rubb'd in a Mortar to a fine Powder.[17]

The two powders were then mixed together, and taken three times a day 'in a large Tea-cup full of white wine, Cyder, or Punch ... These Medicines do frequently cause much Pain at first,' warns Mrs Stephens, 'in which case it is proper to give an Opiate, and repeat it as often as there is occasion.' Never mind the kidney stones: this was, quite simply, a recipe for money.

Sarah Mapp was an altogether different sort of quack. She first emerges as Sarah Wallin in Wiltshire, the strong and stocky daughter of a bone-setter, with more spirit than was good for her. She was restless and ambitious; as soon as was practicable she left home and began to tour southern England, no doubt armed with the nostrums and potions necessary for efficacious quackery, and eventually settled in Epsom, Surrey, in about 1730.

Epsom was a fashionable place, and close enough to London to be attractive to the sort of 'quality' with money enough to divide their lives – or their families – between town and country. Sarah, on the other hand, now calling herself 'Crazy Sally the bone-setter', was coarse, fat and startlingly ugly, with bulbous eyes and a nose that must have rivalled Mother Shipton's for size and luminosity.

Yet she was an enormous success. With her 'extraordinary neat' strapping and her brute but elegantly precise ability to wrench dislocations and fractures back into line, Crazy Sally attracted a clientele to Epsom ranging 'from the lowest labourer to those of the most exalted rank and situation'; so grateful was the town for the custom and renown she brought it that it offered her an honorarium of 300 guineas just to stay there – a vast sum of money in those days. And that was on top of her fees. A reporter for the *London Magazine* marvelled at this

> young woman in Epsom, who though not very regular, it
> is said, in her conduct, has wrought such cures as seem

[55]

miraculous in the bone-setting way . . . and 'tis reckoned she gets near 20 guineas a day.[18]

Success, of course, breeds success. Once Sarah's fame spread to London, there was no stopping her. At first she used to travel up twice a week, to hold clinics in that ultra-fashionable haunt of scientists and savants, the Grecian Coffee-House in Devereux Street, off the Strand. When her patients became too numerous and exalted for her to manage there, she set herself up with consulting-rooms in Pall Mall. She raked it in, and, what's more, her so-called quackery actually worked.

Crazy Sally savoured the absurd celebrity of her life. She used to drive about London in a chariot drawn by four horses and attended by liveried outriders. On one occasion she was apparently mistaken, in all her pomp and glory, for a particularly unpopular lady of the German aristocracy visiting the capital at the time; as crowds gathered around the chariot to jeer at her and lob tomatoes, she tore aside the curtains and bawled out of the window: 'Damn your bloods. Don't you know me? I'm Mrs Mapp the bone-setter!'[19] The jeers soon turned to uproarious cheers, as Crazy Sally was sent on her way.

One of the highlights of her career was the first performance of a play, rather disconcertingly entitled *The Husband's Relief*, performed in her honour at Lincoln's Inn Fields. It included the following ditty, no doubt enjoyed by Sarah:

> You surgeons of London who puzzle your pates
> To ride in your coaches and purchase estates
>   Give over for shame for your pride has a fall,
> For ye doctress of Epsom has outdone you all,
>   Derry down . . .
>
> Dame nature has given her a doctor's degree,
> She gets all the patients and pockets the fee;
>   So if you don't instantly prove her a cheat

'next door to the King's Arms Tavern at Fleet Bridge' in 1702.[23] In America, on the other hand, there were seventy-eight colonial papers in circulation during the seventeenth century, of which sixteen were edited by women.[24] In fact the first American printing-press of all, set up in Cambridge, Massachusetts, in 1638, was owned by a woman.[25]

To digress a moment, it is so refreshing to realize that while their contemporaries were still wading through a morass of precedent and expectation at home in Europe, those women who ventured out to the colonies were often able to set their own precedent as far as work was concerned. There were jobs to be done and not enough men to do them all, so women did them instead. A quick trawl through the records of the southern colonies of America during the eighteenth century[26] reveals an exhilarating range of occupations and responsibilities held by women: Mary Stevenson was a glazier and painter in South Carolina in 1735; Jane Inch was a silversmith in Maryland and Mary Willett a pewterer in the 1760s and 1770s. Elizabeth Russell was a shipwright, and Cassandra Ducker the owner and manager of a fulling mill, where cloth was cleansed and thickened, again in Maryland. Jane Massey was a gunsmith; Ann Lynes a ferry-keeper; Elizabeth Skinner one of several plantation-owners and tobacco-planters: the list goes on and on.

There were a few eccentric but still respectable and authoritative women working in the 'old country' too, of course, in areas that before had been the traditional province of men. Constance Pley was one of them: a Dorset woman, described by her local Member of Parliament as 'as famous a she-merchant as you have met with in England, one who turns and winds thirty-thousand pounds a year.'[27] She went into business as sailcloth, hemp and cordage supplier first to Cromwell's navy and then to the Crown's. Samuel Pepys, in his official capacity in the naval office, knew and admired Mrs Pley for both her efficiency and her tenacity; she was a person for whom business was, quite simply, her 'sole delight in this world'.

Joan Dant (*c.*1631–1715) was a woman after Constance's heart: she was a Quaker, the widow of a Spitalfields weaver, who set herself up after her husband's death as a pedlar in hosiery and haberdashery. She needed to earn a living but ended up earning a fortune. From selling from a box on her back, door to door, she progressed to dealing wholesale; eventually she established a far-reaching import/export business based in London, Brussels and Paris, and when she died she left the staggering sum of £9,000. 'I got it by the rich,' she said, 'and I mean to leave it to the poor' – which she did.[28]

Another entrepreneur I should dearly love to know more about is the Orkney wind-seller Bessy Miller. Bessy is noted in a book about women and the sea[29] as being the last of a long line of Orcadian wind-sellers, willing to promise the finest breeze for anywhere on earth, given the money. She does not seem to have been considered a witch, merely as someone with a valuable gift, providing a very specific service for those in need of it. With her colleagues on the mainland of Scotland, in Finland and in Lapland, she catered for a gap in the market, and prospered.

It is good to know about these unorthodox and accomplished ladies. They are amongst the first independent, named women in history to be remembered objectively for what they did – rather than for who they were (i.e. who their male relations were), or for how they behaved (i.e. how healthy their morality was). Before this pre-revolutionary period, they would have been condemned for being different: eccentricity was too often indistinguishable from iniquity. It is a prejudice historians still suffer from: Mrs Phelps, for all her flair in establishing a mail order business (and choosing such an innovative product!) is still regarded as little more than a back-street quack. Sarah Mapp herself resorted to a technique perfected in the Victorian age by acknowledging herself 'Crazy Sally' to forestall accusations of taking herself too seriously. Many of the printers and publishers of the time are celebrated not for the effort involved in their achievements, but for the unwomanly conviction of their beliefs and the most contentious of their works.

What characterizes this age, as far as I'm concerned, is the impression that women were slowly beginning to choose *not* to be domestic anonymities, but to reach for some personal fulfilment in their working lives, without being considered heretical for doing so. They 'shifted it', as the author of the *Lawes Resolutions* would put it, with both probity and panache, which is a combination not often awarded before to ordinary women. In fact panache – infamy, even – was much more popular a trait than probity during the late seventeenth and early eighteenth centuries. In an age of caricature and burlesque, ideally suited to the dimensions and demeanour of Sarah Mapp, who was sketched both by Cruikshank and by Hogarth,[30] it is perhaps inevitable that the public imagination, then and now, should be attracted by those women who populate what one author has called the underside of history.[31] There has always been something titillating about a woman wilfully mortgaging her femininity (and all the virtues that femininty confers) to be bad.

The feminist in me thinks this unfair; at the same time I feel, slightly shame-facedly, drawn to the more wayward ladies of the period who shifted it well enough, but did not bother much with probity. They are too good to miss.

So meet Catherine Deshayes de Monvoisin (died 1680), immortalized as 'La Voisin', a professional poisoner, who sold her noxious arsenical potions, enterprisingly advertised as 'inheritance powders', to the jealous ladies of the court of Louis XIV. After being tried for playing a material part in the so-called Poison Affair of 1679, which involved the convenient deaths of those assorted husbands and notaries standing in the way of Louis and his mistresses, La Voisin was convicted as a witch, and burned.

Elizabeth Chudleigh (1720–88) was more of a speculator. She

was an English adventuress, successively (or concurrently) maid of honour to Augusta, Princess of Wales, wife, mistress and heiress to several members of the British aristocracy, a bigamist, a bank-robber (once demanding money at gunpoint in Rome for her passage back to England for a court case), and finally a brandy-distiller in St Petersburg, before retiring to a sybaritic life on the Continent, luxuriating in the fruits of her labour – an enterprising lady if ever there was one.

Then there is Mary Young, or 'Jenny Diver', an Irish girl hanged at Tyburn in 1740 for her prowess as a pick-pocket, fraudster and London gangland leader. *The Newgate Calendar*, an eighteenth-century dictionary of the infamous prison's most notorious inmates, introduced her thus:

> A character more skilled in the various arts of imposition and robbery we cannot expect to present to our readers than that of Mary Young. Her depredations, executed with the courage of a man, and the softer deceptions of an artful female surpass any thing which we have, as yet, come to in our researches into crimes and punishments . . .[32]

Mary's modus operandi as Jenny Diver the thief was simple, probably unprecedented, and sensationally efficient:

> . . . she procured a pair of false hands to be made; and concealing her real ones under her clothes, she then put something beneath her stays to make herself appear as if in a state of pregnancy; she repaired on a Sunday evening to the [church], in a sedan chair, one of the gang going before, to procure a seat among the genteeler part of the congregation, and another attending in the character of a footman.
>
> Jenny being seated between two elderly ladies, each of

whom had a gold watch by her side, she conducted herself with great seeming devotion; but when the service was nearly concluded, she seized the opportunity, when the ladies were standing up, of stealing their watches, which she delivered to an accomplice in an adjoining pew. The devotions being ended, the congregation were preparing to depart, when one of the ladies discovered their loss, and a violent clamour ensued: one of the injured parties exclaimed that 'her watch must have been taken either by the devil or the pregnant woman;' on which the other said she 'could vindicate the pregnant lady, whose hands, she was sure, had not been removed from her lap during the whole time of being in the pew'.[33]

Jenny was caught in the end, though, and after twice being transported to Virginia, and twice more resorting to her dangerous craft, she was sentenced to death by hanging, and her life 'was resigned as a sacrifice to those laws which she had so daringly violated.'

The American Mary Butterworth (1685–1775) was too canny ever to be convicted. She was so assiduous a counterfeiter that she went to the trouble of inventing a means of printing bills of credit – imperceptibly fakes – without the need of a copper engraving plate. She went on to set up a cottage industry of friends and family literally churning out money on their kitchen tables during the early 1720s. She included the town clerk of her home in Massachusetts and a County Court judge amongst her homeworkers – which may well be why she was acquitted, when arrested under suspicion in 1723, due to lack of evidence.

There was plenty of evidence to convict the infamous women pirates Ann Bonny and Mary Read at their trial in Jamaica three years earlier. It was scintillating stuff, with numerous witnesses, male and female, swearing to outrage after outrage at the hands of these brazen buccaneers. They 'wore Mens Jackets, and Long

Trouzers, and Handkerchiefs tied about their Heads, and . . . each of them had a Machet[e] and Pistol in their Hands'. They cursed and drank, stamping about the deck 'willing to do any Thing' and ready, at all times, for murder. What is more, they 'did not seem to be kept, or detain'd by Force', but operated 'of their own Free-Will and Consent.'[34]

Mary and Ann's story is a complicated one. Both were brought up as boys. Mary had masqueraded as her own half-brother, who, unknown to his grandparents (whose heir he was), had died in infancy. Her enterprising mother, when widowed, passed Mary off as him, thus assuring and duly appropriating his inheritance. This suited the girl well, according to Daniel Defoe, who wrote up her life and Ann Bonny's in his *General History of the Robberies and Murders of the most notorious Pyrates* (1724),[35] she was 'bold and strong' and had a 'roving mind'; as soon as she was old enough she ran away to sea, signing up as crew on a man of war. Defoe takes up the story:

> [Next] she went over into Flanders, and carry'd Arms in a Regiment of Foot, as a Cadet; and tho' upon all Actions she behaved herself with a great deal of Bravery, yet she could not get a Commission, they being generally bought and sold; therefore she quitted the Service, and took on in a Regiment of Horse; she behaved so well in several Engagements, that she got the Esteem of all her Officers; but her Comrade, who was a Fleming, happening to be a handsome young Fellow, she falls in Love with him, and from that Time, grew a little more negligent in her Duty, so that, it seems, Mars and Venus could not be served at the same time . . . Love is ingenious, and as they lay together in the same Tent, and were constantly together, she found a Way of letting him discover her Sex, without appearing that it was done by design.

He was much surprized at what he found out, and not
a little pleased . . .[36]

The two soldiers duly married, and Mary – reinvented for
a while as a woman – set up the Three Horseshoes, an inn
and eating-house, near Breda in the Netherlands. Sadly, Mary's
husband died before they had a chance to amass any savings, and
after re-enlisting for a while in Holland, Mary returned to the sea,
this time on a privateer bound for the West Indies.

Ann, meanwhile, had grown up near Cork in Ireland, illegitimate
but well loved by her lawyer father, who took her to live with him
disguised as a boy to avoid the scandal of acknowledging his
bastard, known by everyone locally to have been born a girl.
Ann's father emigrated to Carolina during her childhood, and
no doubt despaired of his wayward daughter, once (erroneously)
reputed to have knifed an English serving-maid to death and beaten
a would-be lover so robustly 'that he lay ill of it a considerable
time'. Her father cherished hopes of making a profitable match
for his daughter, who had thrown off her disguise, we assume,
on the voyage to Carolina. Ann would have none of it, though,
and eloped with 'a young Fellow, who belong'd to the Sea, and
was not worth a Groat.'

The newly-weds settled on the island of New Providence in the
Bahamas, where Ann first came across the pirate captain Jack
Rackam, known as Calico Jack for the smart cotton jacket he
wore, sewn by his lover, somewhat improbably named Pierre the
Pansy Pirate.[37] Ann was entranced, and left her husband to go
to sea, donning black velvet breeches glistening with silver coins
down the seams (the handiwork of Pierre again), and happy, one
imagines, for the first time in her life.

Ann and Mary met in 1718, when Mary's privateer was seized
by Jack and Ann's vessel in the Caribbean, and after some awk-
ward moments of discovering each other's sex, the two forged
a powerful partnership. They wore women's weeds when things

[65]

were quiet, but were quick to change to battledress when the fun began.

On 5 September 1720, a proclamation was issued by Woodes Rogers, Governor of the Bahamas, declaring the now notorious Jack Rackam and his crew to be officially 'Enemies to the Crown of Great Britain'. It detailed the names of Rackam's pirates, including 'Two women, by name Ann Fulford alias Bonny, & Mary Read.' Elsewhere they were described as 'spinsters of Providence Island ... proved to have taken an active part in piracies, wearing men's clothes and armed.' Their ship was captured soon afterwards, and the trial that followed was a local sensation.

The penalty for piracy at that time was death by hanging. Mary and Ann, however, made an unprecedented plea in the annals of piracy by declaring themselves to be pregnant, and thus immune (for a while) from the terminal sentence. The records of what happened to them in the end are rather scant, but Mary seems to have died of fever in jail before her baby was born, while Ann gave birth and then promptly disappeared from history. Perhaps she died in childbirth, or escaped, or was hanged after all. Alas, no one knows.

Breathtakingly unconventional as Mary's and Ann's exploits were, even they could not 'roar' quite as boisterously as someone they would no doubt have heard of in their youth: Merry 'Cutpurse' Moll. Moll, or more properly Mary Frith, was born to 'good and tender' parents in Aldgate, London, in 1584.[38] Her father was a cobbler, and both he and his wife were anxious that their fine and lusty daughter should grow up neat, demure and useful to the man she would marry. But Mary, they had to acknowledge, was a handful: 'a very tomrig and rumplescuttle she was,' given to fighting with boys, and roaming the streets of London in 'a boisterous and masculine spirit,' accompanied by her dreadful mastiff, Wildbrat. She was intractable, lewd, plain and brawny, with 'a natural abhorrence to children': not ideally equipped for the marriage market. Besides, Mary had grander ideas: she used to bore people witless with tales of how she planned to sail to America and make her fortune in the abundant gold and silver mines she imagined to be there. In fact, so exasperated did her friends become that they inveigled her down to the docks at Gravesend one day, got her drunk, and smuggled her on board a ship about to embark for the New World. Mary came round just in time to realize where she was, that she did not want to be there after all, and that if she were quick, she could escape – which she did by jumping overboard and swimming to the shore.

Having committed herself to her home city, Mary considered her career. She never entertained the idea of petty crime: she had bigger ambitions, and a penchant for extremes. So she decided to set up a 'factory', two doors away from the Globe Tavern in Fleet Street, where she would receive stolen goods and then return them to their owners – for a fee. When one busybody turned up to claim a gold watch with a constable in tow, and Mary was arrested, she simply arranged for a friend to steal the watch again from the constable's pocket in court, so that when the vital evidence was called for, it was gone. Mary went free.

She was arrested again in 1612 for 'immodest behaviour' (she was famous for her love of alcohol, and revelled in regarding herself as the first woman in England to smoke a pipe). This time she was convicted, and sentenced to 'stand and do penance in a white sheet at Paul's Cross during morning sermon on a Sunday.' Ever the exhibitionist, she armed herself for the occasion by knocking back six pints of Spanish wine, and thoroughly enjoyed the show.

Anecdotes of Mary abound: she once took a bet of £20 to ride from Charing Cross to Shoreditch 'astraddle on horseback in breeches and doublet', blaring a trumpet as she went. She enjoyed wearing men's clothes: they were comfortable, negated her sex, immoral, and were not worn by other women, which would have been a good enough reason on its own. On another occasion, a friend stuffed gunpowder in her pipe instead of tobacco, and to celebrate Charles I's return from France in 1638, being a staunch Royalist, she ordered the open drain in the street outside her home to be filled with wine.

Mary did not like to confine herself too closely in what she called her 'vocation' of being the governess of London's underworld. She worked on the shop-floor occasionally, picking pockets and slashing purses with the best of them. She enjoyed highway robbery particularly, once having the satisfaction of holding up the Roundhead General Fairfax on Hounslow Heath, shooting him through the arm, and relieving him of two of his horses. This escapade resulted in her being tried and condemned at Newgate, but a timely (and staggeringly generous) bribe to the prison officer of £2,000 ensured that she was not detained long. Merry Moll said afterwards that Ralph Briscoe, the clerk of Newgate Prison, was the only man she would ever have considered marrying (except that she didn't put it quite like that: he was the only man she might have 'hired . . . to my embraces').

Moll deliberately kept her sexuality a mystery. She always claimed that she would die a virgin, and however happy she was to pimp for friends and clients (her neat and genteely furnished home in Fleet Street, full of much-loved dogs and parrots, acted as 'a double temple of Priapus and Venus'), she seems to have prided herself in never submitting to anyone. She advertised her establishment as a brothel, not only for gentlemen but for ladies too, and was happy to cater for all tastes.

Hardly surprisingly, Moll really was a legend in her own lifetime. *The Madde Pranckes of Merry Moll* features in a bookseller's catalogue of 1610, although no copy appears to be extant now. A year later came Thomas Middleton's and Thomas Dekker's play *The Roaring Girle*, and in 1662, three years after her death, Moll's (surely ghosted) autobiography was incorporated into *The Life and*

Death of Mrs Mary Frith, which soon became, like the play and the woman herself, a roaring success.

To close Mary's story, here are a couple of quotes from *The Life and Death. . .* The first illustrates her strenuous idiosyncracy:

> My devices were all of my own spinning, nor was I beholding to any stale artifice whatsoever of any woman preceding me.[39]

And the last, worthy of a woman whose laugh 'echoed round half London', was her final joke:

> Let me be lain in my grave on my belly, with my breech upwards, as well for a lucky resurrection at doomsday, as because I am unworthy to look upwards, and that as I have in my life been preposterous, so may I be in my death.[40]

Someone else who had seen the inside of a prison in her time – and knew how to please an audience – was the Royalist spy turned playwright, Aphra Behn. Born Aphra Johnson near Canterbury, Kent, in 1640, she was the daughter of a barber and a wet-nurse (though nothing seems too certain about her early life). One of her mother's professional charges was Thomas Colepeper, the son of local gentry, whom Aphra called her foster-brother. Thomas and his family took the lively young Aphra under their wing, introducing her as she grew older to literary and political friends in London, and encouraging her striking 'apartness'. For when Aphra went to church, it was not out of a sense of duty or devotion, like other girls, but because she enjoyed working out the probable or potential sexual liaisons of various members of the congregation, herself included. She adored the current high fashion for Arcadian romances, and looked for a life of romantic adventure she doubted Kent could offer.

The next we hear of her, in the autobiographical elements of her short story *Oroonoko, or, The Royal Slave* (1688), she is sailing away in about 1663 to the crack of her lovers' breaking hearts,[41] to Surinam, between the Orinoco and the Amazon rivers of South America. By this account, her father, as a result of distant aristocratic connections, had been appointed Lieutenant-General of Surinam and the thirty-six islands off its coast, but had died on the voyage out. When the rest of the family arrived, all they could do, in a territory now dangerously close to capitulation to the Dutch enemy, was wait for the next ship home.

This story about her father is somewhat dubious: what seems much more likely now is that Aphra travelled as a companion to the Lieutenant-General's family (whose name is unrecorded), or else as a governess, or even – given what came later – a spy. The next episode in Aphra's life involved marriage to a German or Dutch merchant or slaver in about 1664 or 1665, whom she may have met on the voyage home to London; he evaporated soon after her arrival in London, though, probably a victim of the plague, leaving Aphra free to stride pastures new.

Soon afterwards came the adventure that intrigues me the most: Mrs Behn became a secret agent in the pay of the King. In Surinam she had made a point of befriending one William Scot, an English exile whose father Thomas had been in charge of Cromwell's intelligence service before being executed at the restoration of Charles II. William had been on his father's staff, and fled to Surinam on his death to try to raise a revolt against the King amongst the colony's disaffected (and the Dutch). Aphra's and William's relationship was a very public one: the Deputy Governor called them Astrea and Celadon, after the besotted heroes of a popular romance of the time.[42] Indeed, it has been mooted that even then Aphra was involved in espionage, assiduously setting a honey-trap for Scot, but if so, it didn't work.

Astrea is the name Aphra adopted when sent on her first properly documented mission to Holland in 1666. By now Britain was at war with the Dutch, and Scot had hinted at a caucus of republican dissenters gathering in Antwerp to prepare a new rebellion. Aphra, as a poor widow, needed work, and possibly applied to the Colepepers for help, which resulted in her appointment as a spy.

Her brief was to travel to Flanders as a lady of quality, with her younger brother and an elderly maid for cover; to seek out and seduce Scot into betraying the traitors and their plans; and to report home frequently and fully in a code she had to memorize before leaving London.[43] She was given £50 to cover her initial expenses, with the promise of more once she produced some result. But she was cheated out of about £10 when she exchanged her sterling for guilders as soon as she arrived in Antwerp; keeping her numerous party with a roof over its head and food in its mouth was a far costlier business, at £1 per day, than she had imagined, and soon she was reduced to pawning jewellery and writing increasingly desperate letters home to her 'control', pleading for more money – without success.

Scot was not much use, either: he was arrested by the Dutch before Aphra could drain him of all the information she needed, and although she was collecting good and useful intelligence elsewhere (warning of an imminent Dutch invasion of London by way of the Thames) she could not afford to stay in the field and, over £100 in debt by now, she came home exhausted and exceedingly angry.

She spent the next few months petitioning for her fees and expenses from the King, but to no avail. Everyone at court was too slippery, passing on the responsibility for paying her to someone else, until the poor woman was imprisoned as a debtor in about 1668. This seems to have been the spur for her change of career: so desperate was she to make a living that she decided to prostitute her muse, and sell her herself in print.[44]

The rest is well known. As the author of some fifteen coarse and clever plays, numerous romantic novels, and finely wrought poems, Aphra Behn became the first professional woman writer in England. 'I write for bread,' she said proudly, and as she wrote well, she earned well. When she died in 1689 she was buried in Westminster Abbey, and is remembered today as remarkable not just as a woman, but for her work too. And though doubtless an efficient agent as 'Astrea', it seems unlikely she would have found the fame and celebration she so enjoyed had she stayed behind the scenes to play the spy.

What characterized the successful women of this age for me was chiefly their inability to stay in the background of daily life. And while most of them were probably only interested in self-fulfilment, others were making a definite political point as they thrust themselves into the comparative limelight, whether as heroines or villainesses. Joan Dant addressed herself to the redistribution of wealth. Mrs Baldwin was an evangelist for the republican cause, while cavalier Moll – 'honest Moll', some called her – shocked a complacent public by kicking everyone's idea of womanly propriety into the gutter, and getting on with enjoying life. She had her own perverse integrity, and integrity invites respect.

I think it unlikely, though, that many of these women would be prepared to stand as role models, or that they chose a career for themselves to encourage other women to do the same. Even Christine de Pizan recognized that she was a one-off (although she was intent on persuading women to believe in themselves as she had done, and to demand wider opportunities and the education to take advantage of them). It is not until we get to the theorists of the late seventeenth and early eighteenth centuries, who for various reasons could afford the time and energy to discuss the position of modern women in print, that we begin to sense that women were at last gaining confidence to change not only themselves, but the world as well.

4

PETTICOTERIES

Now let enfranchiz'd Ladies learn to write,
And not Paint white, and red, but black, and white.
Their Bodkins turn to Pens, to Lines their Locks,
And let the Inkhorn be their Dressing-box.
                                        Anon.[1]

THIS CHAPTER INVOLVES A SHIFT IN LOCATION from the raucous
streets of Moll Cutpurse and her kind to the altogether seemlier
milieu of the drawing room and, perhaps, a shift in emphasis too,
from what is done to what is said.

We are still in the seventeenth and eighteenth centuries, though,
an era of wild contrasts, when on the one hand women were still
being denounced with medieval vitriol, while on the other literary
ladies were encouraged (within reason) to engage in a new era of
enlightenment. The vitriol erupted in laws like this one, against
the general perfidy of the sex:

> ... all women of whatever age, rank, profession or
> degree, whether virgin, maid or widow, that shall from
> and after [this] Act, impose upon, seduce, and betray
> into matrimony any of His Majesty's subjects by means

of scent, paints, cosmetics, washes, artificial teeth, false
hair, Spanish wool, iron stays, hoops, highheeled shoes,
or bolstered hips, shall incur the penalty of the Law now
in force against witchcraft and like misdemeanour . . .[2]

Meanwhile, the Age of Reason was dawning, and reason-
able ladies were finding themselves discontent to sit at home
decorating themselves, playing cards, or doing decoupage while
their menfolk deliberated in the coffee-houses or elsewhere. So
discussion groups of wives and daughters began to emerge,
social sisterhoods, or 'petticoteries', as Horace Walpole somewhat ungallantly put it, whose keen, frustrated minds began
to turn to an examination of their current and future political
state. Female education (or the lack of it) was debated as
were emotional and economic oppression and opportunities for
fulfilling practical and intellectual needs: the seeds of feminism
were thus being sown.

This is not intended to be a book about feminism, but it
does acknowledge what women have felt themselves able to do,
throughout history, despite a perceived lack of opportunity and
support. That said, I do think it is important also to recognize that
by the middle of the eighteenth century there was an intellectual
movement afoot (politically stymied, of course), aimed at creating
the sort of world in which ladies might be equipped to choose
a stimulating, useful and rewarding life – working, or otherwise.
As yet, the petticoteries were only interested in 'ladies' as opposed
to lower-class 'women'. And no doubt these lower classes took
no notice of the petticoteries' pontifications. But, especially with
regard to women's education, what these enlightened ladies had
to say was prescient, and what some of them did in support of
their beliefs was both admirable and (eventually) influential.

It was the custom, come the end of the seventeenth century, to
celebrate the fashionable dead by publishing volumes of panegyric
on the unsurpassable quality of their learning, their wit, their

generosity, or (if female) their ability to marry well and produce an abundance of sound and sturdy children. Margaret Cavendish, Duchess of Newcastle, died in 1674, and sure enough, two years later, *Letters and Poems in Honour of the Incomparable Princess, Margaret, Dutchess of Newcastle* was published, bursting with praise for the noble lady's accomplishments. She did not leave a legacy of heirs, but had certainly excelled in the other categories:

> None was more good, and once none was more fair:
> She was not as most of her frail Sex are;
> Who'ave Fruitful Wombs but Barren Brains,
> She left the best Remains:
> Though we no Issue of her Body find
> Yet she hath left behind
> The Nobler Issue of her mighty Mind.[3]

Often eulogies such as these were merely a matter of political posturing; in Margaret Cavendish's case, however, the poet was right. She did have a mighty mind, one which drove her, as another poet put it, to 'Scale the walls of Fame'[4] to seek success.

The Duchess was not so much acclaimed for how well she wrote, as for how loudly. She produced a substantial and belligerent body of literature, in which she subverted the cosmetic vogue of the day by writing as she thought. She thought other women silly, stupid even, especially when pregnant (a state she did not achieve herself). She was splenetic about the great-bellied complacence of the *enceinte*, with all their sickly airs and graces, 'rasping wind out of [their] stomache' all day long and swooning about the place. She deplored the ubiquitous feminine obsession with romantic love, having never (thankfully) been 'infected' by it herself and enjoying instead a mutually respectful and supportive friendship with the Duke, her husband. He allowed her to write with impunity, not even minding when she put her name to the essays,

poems, letters, biography and even the autobiography she published (acknowledged authorship for a lady being thought vulgar
and low). Nor did the dear chap object when his wife published a
series of *Orations of Divers Persons* (1662), arguing for freedom
of speech and education for women. She prided herself, after all,
on her eccentricity, and being an aristocratic eccentric, she was
regarded fondly and indulged.

Margaret's literary output heralded a strange and uncomely
breed of eighteenth-century women, celebrated – or ridiculed
– for their intellectual earnestness. The original Bluestockings
were privately educated ladies (courtesy of a tutor, a 'tutoress',
or perhaps one of those very expensive boarding-schools, like
Ladies' Hall in Deptford, London, which opened in 1617) who
had the time, the means and the intellectual inclination to think
radically.

One particular petticoterie, led by the literary patron and critic
Elizabeth Montagu (1720–1800), whom Samuel Johnson called
'the Queen of the Blues', used to meet regularly at salons in
London and Bath to discuss 'bon ton'[5] and the politics of the
oppressed, amongst whom, as women, they counted themselves.
Guests were encouraged never to dress in a way that compromised
comfort and individuality, nor to lisp or totter and counterfeit the
usual feminine weaknesses supposed so attractive to gentlemen.
One (ironically, a man)[6] went so far one evening as to come clad
not in customary black silk hose, but in shocking blue woollen
stockings. It was this sartorial idiosyncracy which caught the
public imagination more than any intellectual radicalism, and
ever since the term 'Bluestocking' has been taken to mean a
woman (exclusively) so beguiled by her own brains as not to
care how she looks. A ridiculous *Femme Savante*,[7] as Molière
would have her – a freak.

At the time however, the Bluestockings were debating live and
pertinent issues, especially the advisability of women's education.
Traditionally, of course, women-in-general were dissuaded by

De serpente decipiente adam et euam. Gen. iii.

The moment of damnation: Eve hands the forbidden fruit to Adam.
Even the serpent in this medieval Garden of Eden is female

Three vignettes of working women from Renaissance manuscripts:
a teacher (*above left*), a mural painter (*above right*) and a jeweller (*below*)

Christine de Pizan (c.1364-1430), professional writer and
advocate of financial independence for women

The Strange and Wonderful HISTORY
OF
𝕸other 𝕾hipton,

Plainly ſetting forth

Her prodigious Birth, Life, Death, and Burial.

With an exact Collection of all her famous

PROPHECYS

More Compleat than ever yet before published. And large Explanations, shewing how they have all along been fulfilled to this very YEAR.

Licenſed according to Order.

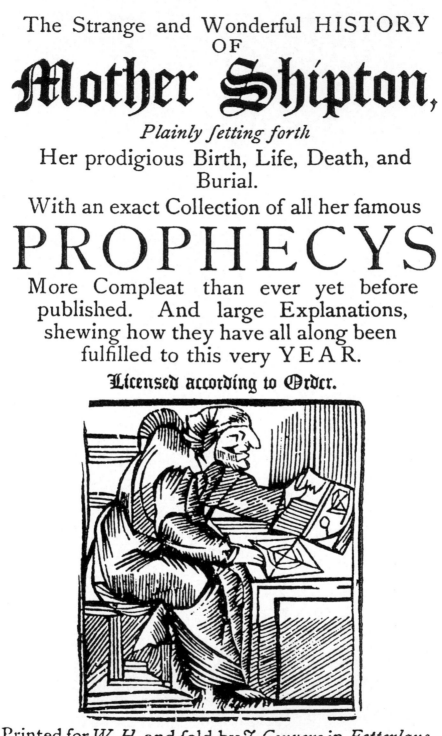

Printed for *W.H.* and ſold by *J. Conyers* in *Fetterlane.*
1686.

Prophetess Ursula Sontheil's life-story and 'sayings'. She was popularly known as Mother Shipton, and remains one of Britain's most famous seers

The Roaring Girle.

OR
Moll Cut-Purse.

As it hath lately beene Acted on the Fortune-stage by
the Prince his Players.

Written by *T. Middleton* and *T. Dekker.*

My case is alter'd, I must worke for my living.

Printed at *London* for *Thomas Archer,* and are to be sold at his
shop in Popes head-pallace, neere the Royall
Exchange. 1611.

Middleton's and Dekker's play about the outrageous Mary Frith, or Moll Cutpurse,
celebrated one of history's feistiest career women

Eighteenth–century pirates Mary Read and Ann Bonny in the Caribbean

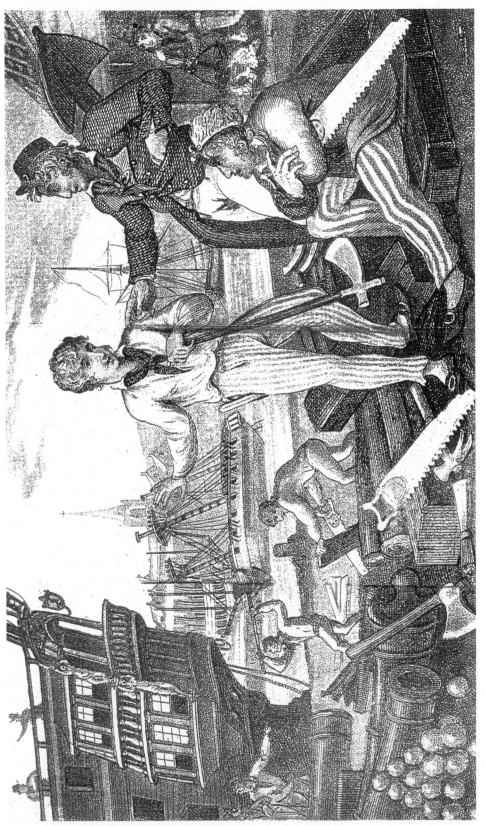

Mary Lacey, the female shipwright, at work in Portsmouth Dockyard

(*Top*) Astronomer Caroline Herschel at ninety-two, as proud of her ability to earn (and spend) her own money as of her scientific achievements

(*Middle*) Loreta Janeta Velasquez wears the medal she won on active service as Lieutenant Harry T. Buford during the American Civil War

(*Bottom left*) Hannah Snell (1723–92), who graduated from infantryman to Royal Marine

men-in-general from bothering with learning for learning's sake
at all:

> All things of an abstracted nature are Incomprehen-
> sible to them. They cannot employ their Imagination in
> disentangling compound and perplex'd Questions. Their
> consideration terminates on the surface and outside of
> things; and their imagination has neither Strength nor
> Reach enough to pierce to the bottom of them ... In
> short, the Mode and not the Reality of things, is enough
> to take up the whole Capacity of their Mind.[8]

The Bluestockings would parry that women like them had
already begun to excel, especially in the fertile fields of science
and natural history. Think of Montaigne's adopted daughter
Marie le Jars de Gournay (1566–1645), who wrote impassioned
pleas for women to be treated as the intellectual equals of
men,[9] and would, had the term existed, have been proud to
call herself a feminist. Or the French mining engineer Martine
de Bertereau du Châtelet (died 1642), who wrote treatises on
metallurgy and hydraulics. Lady Anne Conway (1631–79) was
a mathematician, astronomer, author of *The Principles of the
Most Ancient and Modern Philosophy* (posthumously published
in 1690), and so keen an experimental chemist that she had a
laboratory installed at Ragley Hall, her home. Then there was
the Italian mathematician, Maria Agnesi (1718–99), the eldest of
twenty-one children, mistress of at least five languages by the age
of nine, and who went on to publish a life's work on differential
calculus ...

The prolific English historian, Catherine Macaulay (1731–91),
was a perfect example of the female intellectual: one of the original
Bluestockings, she wrote a vastly popular (and opinionated)
History of England in eight volumes and, according to Mary
Wollstonecraft, was 'the woman of the greatest abilities that

[79]

this country has ever produced.' In fact there were countless literary ladies discussing and dispensing poetry and belles-lettres throughout the civilized world. Had not the time come, at last, to cultivate feminine intellect and bring it to blossom in a better world?

The Duchess of Newcastle certainly thought so. She had no time for girls being left to pick up useful accomplishments either from their mothers and elder sisters, or from fancy schoolmistresses elsewhere: she labelled that sort of teaching as 'women breeding up women; one fool breeding up another; and as long as that custom lasts, there is no hope of amendment.'[10] 'In Nature we have as clear an understanding as Men,' she insisted, 'if we were bred in [proper] Schools to mature our brains.'

Eliza Haywood (1693–1756) was slightly better tempered in her argument for women's education in *The Female Spectator* (a lively periodical she edited herself), widening the issue to take in the common assumption that no woman can concentrate on her mind and her husband at the same time – if she can catch a husband, that is, in the first place:

> ... it is entirely owing to a narrow Education that we either give our Husbands room to find fault with our Conduct, or that we have Leisure to pry too scrutinously into theirs: – Happy would it be for both, were this almost sole Cause of all our Errors once reform'd; and I am not without some Glimmerings of Hope that it will one Day be so. The Ladies themselves, methinks, begin to seem sensible of the Injustice which has long been done them, and find a Vacuum in their Minds, which, to fill up, they, of their own accord, invented the way of sticking little Pictures on Cabinets ... and then varnishing them ... but great Revolutions are not to be expected at once, and if they once take it into their Heads to prefer Works of Ingenuity, tho in the most trifling Matters, to Dress,

Gaming and Rambling Abroad, they will, it is to be hop'd,
proceed to more noble and educated Studies.[11]

All that, of course, is fine for the upper classes. It was generally reckoned, though, that a lady (excepting those precocious
Bluestockings) should not attempt to learn any more than she
needed to give her mind some gentle exercise. As the writer and
traveller Lady Mary Wortley Montagu put it in 1718, fresh from
a disturbingly invigorating three years in Turkey:

> After having read all that is to be found in the languages I
> am mistress of, and having decayed my sight by midnight
> studies, I envy the easy peace of mind of a ruddy
> milkmaid, who, undisturbed by doubt, hears the sermon,
> with humility, every Sunday, not having confounded the
> sentiments of natural duty in her head by the vain enquiries
> of the schools, who may be more learned, yet, after all,
> must remain as ignorant. And, after having seen part of
> Asia and Africa, and almost made the tour of Europe, I
> think the honest English squire more happy, who verily
> believes the Greek wines less delicious than March beer;
> that the African fruits have not so fine a flavour as
> golden-pippins; that the [figs] of Italy are not so well
> tasted as a rump of beef; and that, in short, there is
> no perfect enjoyment of this life out of Old England. I
> pray God I may think so for the rest of my life; and,
> since I must be contented with our scanty allowance
> of day-light, that I may forget the enlivening sun of
> Constantinople.[12]

A little learning is a dangerous thing, said Lady Mary's (incredibly
learned) friend Alexander Pope. And you're not supposed to miss
what you've never had . . .
A little scientific dabbling was fine, though, and fashionable.

[81]

The Ladies Diary of 1716 positively recommended application to 'some Parts of Mathematical Learning amongst the Female Sex', and offered various logical enigmas and riddles to be solved in as pretty a way as possible by its feminine readers. Practicality, however, was vulgar: mental nobility, rather than financial profit, was the aim.

Meanwhile, as usual, women less noble were getting on with an increasingly wide range of practical duties, usually without the benefit of any formal education. An anonymous letter (by 'a Lady') published in *The Gentleman's Magazine* of October 1739, was entitled *A new Method for making Women as useful and as capable of maintaining themselves, as the Men are; and consequently preventing their becoming old Maids, or taking ill Courses*, and rather diffidently advanced a suggestion that all young ladies should enter apprenticeships at the age of fifteen or sixteen. Such a course would stop them becoming giddy (which frequently happened when addled by the elaborate rituals of courtship) or bitter (the inevitable consequence of failing to find a good husband). These apprenticeships should naturally be served only in the seemliest occupations, with 'Linnen or Woollen Drapers, Haberdashers of Small Wares, Mercers, Glovers, Perfumers, Grocers, Confectioners, Retailers of Gold and Silver, Lace, [and] Buttons', and might even result in the reward of 'a handsome and reputable Living, and not [being] forc'd to a disagreeable Match, or even to marry at all . . .'[13]

What that author cannot have realized is that there were women all over the country, and beyond, already engaged in a staggering variety of more or less formal apprenticeships, even during the Industrial Revolution, which herded so many of them from the fields into the factories, and from the back-room loom to the mill.[14] A survey of women's work in eighteenth-century Edinburgh[15] reveals, as well as the usual milliners, mantua-makers, shroud-sewers, and lodging-house keepers, an enterprising array of female shop-owners, auctioneers, brokers, musicians, watch-makers, sugar merchants and travelling saleswomen. In a five-volume *Universal Directory of British Trade* (1790–8) Lucy Burrell the bricklayer is included, as are Mrs Barber the glue-maker, Martha Patinson the plumber and glazier, Mrs Soper the coal merchant, Mrs Haines the carpenter, and Mrs Hayter the farrier and blacksmith.

I doubt if many of these women would have had the time to go to school, and even if they had, few were available. There would be the odd subsidized dame-school in towns and cities, where working parents left their daughters to do a bit of sewing (and perhaps learn to read) until they were old enough to work themselves; there were occasional charity schools set up by the Quakers or other religious bodies dotted around, which took in girls to teach them the basics of morality and literacy as well as practical and domestic accomplishments; otherwise, a vocational education, dictated by family tradition or local circumstances, was all that was on offer. It was not until 1881 that a free, elementary education became compulsory for all girls, from five years old to twelve.

There were stirrings, though, during the period we are talking about: ideological stirrings at first, and then more practical ones, aimed at improving a woman's education and so, by implication, her lot, and ultimately her position in the world. It is impossible to engage in any aspect of British women's history during the eighteenth century without consulting Mary Wollstonecraft, the first great feminist apologist. And there are one or two other figures we should not ignore, whose strident voices have been muffled under layers of literary criticism, biographical analysis and political commentary over the years – Jane Anger or Mary Astell, for example.

Jane Anger (*fl.* 1589) is credited with writing the first published example of what came loosely to be known as a 'Defence'. It was inspired by an 'Attack' (of which, you know by now, there were very many through the years) by Thomas Orwin,[16] which had daintily and brutally listed the usual moral shortcomings and iniquities of woman, and which incensed Jane so deeply that she immediately rattled out her riposte: *Her Protection for Women.*

> Fie on the falsehood of men, whose minds go oft a madding . . . Was there ever any so abused, so slandered, so railed upon, so wickedly handled undeservedly, as are we women. Will the Gods permit it, the Goddesses stay their punishing judgements, and we ourselves not pursue their undoings[?] . . . Let the stones be as Ice, the soles of the shoes as Glass, the moats steep like Aetna, & every blast a whirlwind . . . [to] hasten their passage to the Devils haven . . .[17]

It gets worse, and is never less than invective, but then no one could accuse Jane of mincing her words, and with her, the tradition of whatever is the female equivalent of misogyny was born.

Mary Astell (1666–1731) controlled herself better. Her story is a remarkable one: she was born into a family of merchants – probably in coal – in the north-east of England. Her father died when she was six, and possibly her mother during the sixteen years that passed in historical obscurity before she took herself, alone, to London. There she lived under the patronage of various high-profile, High-Anglican Tories and aristocrats, having bought herself respectability (if not independence) through her writing. She wrote poems and essays, she wrote letters full of passionate discussions on philosophy, theology and ethics, and she wrote *A Serious Proposal to the Ladies.* This was a work issued in two parts (the first in 1694 and Part II three years later), devoted to the mental and political well-being of women.

I suppose Mary earned a living in so much as she attracted patronage: she could not have kept herself, as Aphra Behn did, by the pen, for her writing was too erudite and lacked popular appeal. Her importance, as far as I am concerned, lies in her constant encouragement to women to think for themselves. 'How can you be content to be in the World like Tulips in a Garden,' she asks her lady readers, 'to make a fine shew and be good for nothing?'[18] Why not *do* something instead? Why not join a sisterhood of like-minded women and live together, both mentally and physically self-sufficient? Dowries could be pooled to fund a community, and a school could be set up to bring in an income. If someone wanted to leave, to marry perhaps, they could: there would be no vows, except an implicit vow of self-respect.

Mary did not denigrate marriage, although she herself never chose it: in her *Reflections upon Marriage* (1700 – and it ran into five editions in her lifetime alone) she acknowledged that with due care in the choice of partner, it could be an uplifting and enriching estate. It was usually the very opposite, though, and no woman should feel compelled to mortgage her happiness and moral integrity by submitting to a weak, unworthy husband, according to Mary, even if it meant giving up one's old family and any chance of a new one. After all, 'the whole World is a single Lady's family,' and in a perfect world 'her opportunities of doing good are not lessen'd but encreas'd by her being unconfin'd.'[19]

The *Proposal* made quite an impact on the intellectual audience of the day: its author was either satirized and lampooned, or fêted as one of Britain's foremost philosophers. But the communities she suggested never materialized (even though she did open a charity school in 1709); Miss Astell was an idealist, whose theories were perhaps too revolutionary to be practical.

Mary Ward, of whom Miss Astell (with a devoutly Catholic mother) must have been well aware, was more proactive in pursuing her ends. She was a Yorkshire girl, born in 1585 of a well-connected Catholic family at a time when England was decidedly Protestant. It is not clear how Mary herself was educated, but after the death of her fiancé she is known to have travelled to St Omer in northern France to join the Community of Poor Clares. The neighbouring Low Countries (now Belgium,

Holland and Luxembourg) were refreshingly open then to women keen and able to educate themselves: the spirit of the Counter-Reformation burned brightly there, and soon kindled Mary with a missionary desire to reconvert her homeland to Catholicism through its women.

She dreamed of founding a sort of feminine Society of Jesus, to foster learning, to make women 'cunning', as she put it, in the pursuit of knowledge and therefore of God, and to work amongst themselves to usurp Protestantism. She travelled across the Continent (no mean feat at the time) and back home to England – often without her habit, in plain clothes – to spread the word amongst the legions of 'English Virgins' she hoped to teach. She would call at their houses in clothes anything but plain, actually, expensively arrayed to inspire confidence, and she never lost an opportunity to evangelize for the education of both lay and religious women, insisting that although their provinces in life might, and should, be different, their intellectual capacities, and above all their potential to do good, were the same. 'I hope in God it will be seen that women in time will do much,' she said.[20]

Mary paid for her waywardness. In 1631 her teaching institute, which founded schools in Belgium, Germany, Italy, what is now Austria, and the Czech Republic, was disbanded by Pope Urban VIII. Her methods, involving religious sisters (or 'Galloping Girls', as they were dubbed) working in the world outside the convent, invited suspicion and even contempt from the Vatican. Eventually Mary was arrested for heresy and even, for a while, imprisoned in a dank and tiny cell she called 'my Palace'. Her own 'cunning' spirit was not to be quelled, however; she carried on travelling in Britain and beyond until the end of her life, as an 'enemy of ignorance',[21] with humour as her weapon, determination as her shield, and God, she was sure, on her side.

Mary focused her missionary zeal quite narrowly. Certainly she wanted her English Virgins to flourish individually, but collectively they could do much more with their learning to influence other women, and eventually men, to turn their country back to the true faith. Her target audience primarily comprised the wives and daughters of Catholics wealthy and well-connected enough (like her) to afford an education, which at the end of the sixteenth and the beginning of the seventeenth centuries usually meant venturing abroad to the teaching nunneries of the Netherlands. She was not able to shift the seat of learning to England within her lifetime, but her inspiration meant that girls' schools founded by her Institute of the Blessed Virgin Mary flourish now in countries across the world, including England.

Another ideological pioneer of education for girls was Anna van Schurman (1607–78), who also had strong connections with the more forward-looking Low Countries. Anna was a Protestant, born in Cologne but brought up and educated in Antwerp and Utrecht with her brothers. Her proud father exacted from her a promise never to marry (like Hypatia) and so to preserve the God-given gifts he recognized in her: she was a lutenist, a harpsichordist, a poet and philosopher, a scholar of Latin, Greek, Hebrew, Arabic (et cetera, et cetera), an exquisite embroiderer, draughtswoman, painter and engraver.

It was lucky that she had never been allowed to marry, as it turned out. When her mother died, she was available to run the family household, and in her middle years dropped most of her accomplishments to concentrate on one abiding interest: the female right to an education. In 1650 she published *Whether a Christian Woman Should be Educated* (translated into English in 1659), in which she argued that to deny such women teaching is a sin of omission, it being our duty to worship God with as well-informed a mind as possible. Besides, women have more time to fill than men, she said: they need something worthwhile, something cerebrally nourishing, to occupy what might otherwise be dangerously idle hours.

It is obvious from her arguments that Anna was concerned, as

Mary Astell and Mary Ward were, with gentlewomen. In fact Anna went on to join a Community too, this time founded by French Calvinist Jean de Labadie, whose doctrine was one of 'primitive Christianity'. What mattered to the Labadians was an untutored religious instinct, and Anna soon retracted her former writings on the importance of an intellectual approach to God. Nevertheless she retained to the end of her life a belief that women had as profound a capacity for spirituality as men.

But what this book is really about is practicality. Women like the Duchess of Newcastle, like the Bluestockings, Mary Astell and Mary Ward and Anna van Schurman, were all preparing the ground in an abstract sort of way for the education and therefore the practical empowerment of women; so were the bricklayers and the plumbers and the auctioneers on the other side of the social divide. If one woman was pivotal in beginning to bridge that divide between passive learning and active employment, it must have been the sublimely named (and little-known) Mrs Bathsua Makin.

Once a correspondent of Anna van Schurman (in Greek . . .), Bathsua (*née* Reginald, *c.*1600–*c.*1676) was closely involved in education all her life. And not because it interested her as a concept but because it provided her livelihood. Her father ran a school in London,[22] and not only was she a pupil there herself, but in time she taught there, one of her own pupils considering her 'the greatest scholler, I thinke, of a woman in England'.[23] At the age of about sixteen her first book was published: *Musa Virginea*, a volume of Greek, Latin and French verse. That was her only dalliance in the Arcadian grove, however, for in 1622 she married and settled down to produce at least eleven children and to found schools of her own for girls as well as boys (I should imagine, knowing Bathsua, on equal terms).

Eventually she accepted an appointment as tutor to Charles I's daughter Princess Elizabeth. These were hard times, to put it mildly, for anyone involved with the Royal Household; in 1649 the King was executed, and a year later the young Princess died, leaving Bathsua with no prospect of payment for several years' tutoring fees, and thus in poverty.

Mr Makin had faded from the background, and while relying for support on her brother-in-law, the mathematician John Pell (who had married the even more divinely named Ithamaria Reginald), Bathsua went back to more public teaching and opened a school in Tottenham High Cross in East London. Letters prove that she was still alive in 1675, in her mid seventies, but when she died we don't know. She must have been mourned both as a scholar by her intellectual peers and as an inspirational teacher by her many pupils. Perhaps this extract from her best-known work, *An Essay to Revive the Antient Education of Gentlewomen* (1673), will illustrate her appeal for me:

> Custom, when it is inveterate, has a mighty influence: it has the force of Nature itself. The Barbarous custom to breed Women low is grown general amongst us, and has prevailed so far, that it is verily believed (especially amongst a sort of debauched sots) that Women are not endued with such Reason, as Men; nor capable of improvement by Education, as they are. It is looked upon as a monstrous thing, to pretend to the contrary. A Learned Woman is thought to be a Comet, that bodes Mischief, when ever it appears. To offer to the World the liberal Education of Women is to deface the Image of God in Man, it will make Women so high, and men so low, like Fire in the House-top, it will set the whole world in a Flame . . .
>
> Had God intended Women only as a finer sort of Cattle, he would not have made them reasonable . . . Monkies, (which the Indians use to do many Offices) might have better fitted some men's Lust, Pride, and

Pleasure; especially those that desire to keep them ignorant to be tyrannized over.

God intended Woman as a help-meet to Man, in his constant conversation, and in the concerns of his Family and Estate, when he should most need, in sickness, weakness, absence, death, &c. Whilst we neglect to fit them for those things, we renounce God's Blessing ... are ungrateful to him, cruel to them, and injurious to ourselves.[24]

Bathsua's concern as a highly intelligent teacher was that women's minds should not be wasted: she saw the enforced ignorance of potentially clever girls as a religious and cultural obscenity. As a 'self-sustaining' woman herself, on the other hand, she condemned the lack of opportunities for girls to be the same: 'The end of Learning is to fit one for public Employment.' While I cannot give Mrs Makin all the credit (not knowing the extent of her contemporary readership), it seems to me that from this point on, an educated woman was far more likely to dare not just to think about things, but to do them.

Businesswoman to the last, Bathsua appended an advertisement for her own school to her *Essay to Revive the Antient Art . . .*:

If any inquire where this Education may be performed, such may be informed, That a School is lately erected ... at Tottenham High-Cross, within four miles of London, in the Road to Ware, where Mrs. Makin is Governess, who was sometimes Tutoress to the Princess Elisabeth, Daughter to King Charles the First.

Here, says Bathsua, her girls are taught not only the usual things like dancing, music, singing and writing, but how to keep accounts, how to speak Latin and French, even Greek, Hebrew, Italian and Spanish; they might learn 'the Names, Natures, Values, and Life of Herbs, Shrubs, Trees, Mineral Juices, Metals, and Stones', and 'attain some general Knowledge in Astronomy, Geography . . . Arithmetic, and History' and 'Experimental Philosophy'.

> The Rate shall be [£]20 per annum: But if a competent improvement be made in the Tongues, and the other things aforementioned, as shall be agreed upon, then something more will be expected . . .[25]

It was not quite education for the masses, but a good start: Bathsua wanted to teach so that more and more others might then become teachers themselves.

Even if she was the most trenchant, Bathsua was not the only woman advocating a secular and useful education to others of her sex at the time, nor the only demonstrably learned woman putting such learning to professional use. A contemporary of hers, Hannah Woolley (*c.*1623–*c.*1678), was nothing if not practical, producing a *vade mecum* for the whole of the female sex in *The Gentlewoman's Companion*, published (after seven years in the writing) in 1675.

Hannah's story is recorded by 'A Short Account of the Life and Abilities of the Authoress' included in the *Companion*, in which she tells of her birth in Essex, of her mother's skills 'in Physick and Chyrugery [surgery]', and her being left an orphan while still a girl. She opened her first little school, she says, at the age of fifteen, and because of her obvious talents was engaged at seventeen as a private governess by a generous mistress who taught her cookery and etiquette. With another employer she learned secretarial skills, and 'how to express myself with the attendancy of a becoming air . . . gracefully and discreetly.'[26]

She mentions practising midwifery (as her mother had probably done), and using her various talents and acquired skills to earn herself the dowry denied her by her parents' deaths, before marrying at the age of twenty-four. Her husband was

[91]

a grammar-school master, Benjamin Woolley, and together they ran a boarding-school near Saffron Walden in Essex. In 1655 the family, now including four sons, moved to the village of Hackney, east of London, to set up another school. Sadly, though, Benjamin died six years later, and it was then that Hannah turned to writing.

In 1666 she married again and stopped writing, but in 1674 she was widowed for a second time, and so her prodigious literary output resumed. She wrote about cooking, housekeeping, letter-writing, and even adult and child psychology, but it is the *Companion* that stands as the most eloquent memorial to a practical polymath. Its title (almost) says it all:

> The Gentlewoman's Companion; or, a Guide to the Female Sex: containing Directions of Behaviour, in all Places, Companies, Relations, and Conditions, from their Child-hood down to Old Age: viz, As Children to Parents. Scholars to Governours. Virgins to Suitors. Married to Husbands. Huswifes to the House. Misstresses to the Ser-vants. Mothers to Children. Widows to the World. Prudent to All. With Letters & Discourses upon all Occasions. Whereunto is added, A Guide for Cook-maids, Dairy-maids, Chamber-maids, and all others that go into Service. The Whole being an exact Rule for the Female Sex in General.

This volume will teach you not only the demure significance of 'Gait and Gesture', 'the Government of the Eye' and 'Walking with persons of Honour', but also how to cook a Taffety Tart,[27] a Norfolk Fool, Marinated Mullet, Stewed Pike and 'Pig Roasted with the Hair On'. It gives directions on 'How to order a Woman with Child before, in, and after, the Dilivery [sic]', and – just as usefully – it roundly and cheerfully ridicules the current vogue for what Makin called breeding girls 'low'. 'Most in this depraved later Age think a Woman learned and Wife enough if she can distinguish her Husband's bed from another's,' complains Mrs Woolley. But 'I look upon the end of Life to be Usefulness . . . I have taken great Pains for an honest Livelihood.' She hopes her readers will do the same:

> I cannot but . . . condemn the great negligence of Parents, in letting the fertile ground of their Daughters lie fallow, yet send the barren Noddles of their sons to the University, where they stay for no other purpose than to fill their empty Sconces and make a noise in the Country . . . Vain man is apt to think we were meerly intended for the World's propagation, and to keep its humane inhabitants sweet and clean; but . . . had we the same Literature [i.e. education], they would find our brains as fruitful as our bodies.[28]

It is a shame the author of the Duchess of Newcastle's elegy (also 1674) did not mark that before penning his quip about barren brains and fruitful wombs. For you could hardly find a more useful, enterprising and accomplished person than Hannah Woolley.

Mary Wollstonecraft, that great feminist apologist I mentioned earlier, would have loved to have been useful. She tried to buy her independence as a single woman with a succession of more or less seemly occupations – lady's companion, governess, teacher, editor, translator, writer – and might have succeeded in living the sort of enlightened life she wrote about in her *Vindication of the Rights of Woman* (1792), were it not, ironically, for her emotional dependence on men – and one man in particular. Even though what she wrote is so much more pertinent (in the context of this book) than what she did, hers is such an affecting story that I cannot resist telling it.

Mary was of Irish parentage, born in London in 1759. Her father was a desperate man: a violent alcoholic and a chaser after lost causes. Despite following him to Yorkshire and then to Wales, as he spent his money and health in various (failed) attempts to become a farmer, Mary somehow gleaned herself an education and, when she was nineteen, found work to help support her numerous family and herself as a lady's companion in Bath. Four years later she opened a school back in London and in 1787 published *Thoughts on the Education of Daughters*. The school failed, as did a brief stint as a governess, and by 1790 Mary was working as a publisher's assistant (and was already the author of a novel herself),[29] reading manuscripts and doing a little journalism and translating, while composing furiously at home. Her greatest work at this time was a response to Edmund Burke's *Reflections on the French Revolution* – an extended essay she called *A Vindication of the Rights of Men* (1790).

The revolution profoundly impressed this passionate, radical and free-thinking woman. In researching her *History and Moral View of the Origin and Progress of the French Revolution* (1794) she witnessed not only the political world being turned upside down, but women playing a vital part in the process. Women were leading riots, petitioning for rights, and trying (unsuccessfully, as it turned out) to win a voice in a new world order.[30] It was a frightening, exhilarating, but frustrating experience for Mary.

While she was in France preparing her book on the French Revolution Mary met the American writer, Gilbert Imlay, and began an affair with him which resulted in the birth of a daughter, Fanny. She was infatuated with the man, degradingly beholden to him both emotionally and physically, and when he proved faithless, she twice tried to commit suicide.

In 1795, Mary undertook a commission for her reluctant lover. It involved travelling (alone, save for a long-suffering maid and the baby) to Scandinavia to try to track down a business associate of his, and recover money owed to Imlay. She loved travelling (I think it was one of the few occupations in which she could set her own agenda and live as unconventionally as she wished) and wrote a beautifully bleak account in *Letters Written during a Short Residence in Sweden, Norway, and Denmark* (1796). But the journey could not last for ever: Mary returned to England and eventually settled down with William Godwin, whom she'd known, quietly, for years. She died after giving birth to her second daughter, who was to become Mary Shelley, in 1797.

It was only after her death, when Godwin revealed her unorthodox private life to her reading public, that male critics explicitly equated the supposed laxity of Mary's morals with a corresponding laxity in logical argument. No wonder she has such mad ideas, her character is flawed, they said, she's a Jezebel. Of course, we simply do not know how many women read the impassioned writings of such enemies of ignorance as Wollstonecraft, and of those women who did, how many considered them to have any personal relevance, save as the premise for some stimulating and necessary debate in the petticoteries of Europe and America.[31] To a modern audience her writing seems remarkably fresh: it is salutary stuff, and as England's first true feminist, she deserves to speak for herself.

> I love man as my fellow; but his sceptre, real or usurped, extends not to me, unless the reason of an individual demands my homage; and even then, the submission is to reason, and not to man . . .
>
> Asserting the rights which women in common with men ought to contend for, I have not attempted to extenuate their faults; but to prove them to be the natural consequence of their education and station in society. If so, then it is reasonable to suppose that they will change their character, and correct their vices and

follies, when they are allowed to be free in a physical, moral, and civil sense . . .

[F]emales have been insulated, as it were; and, while they have been stripped of the virtues that should clothe humanity, they have been decked with artificial graces that enable them to exercise a short-lived tyranny. Love [i.e. sentiment] in their bosoms, taking the place of every nobler passion, their sole ambition is to be fair, to raise emotion instead of inspiring respect; and this ignoble desire, like the servility in absolute monarchies, destroys all strength of character. Liberty is the mother of virtue, and if women be, by their very constitution, slaves, and not allowed to breathe the sharp invigorating air of freedom, they must ever languish like exotics, and be reckoned beautiful flaws in nature. Let it also be remembered, that they are the only flaw . . .[32]

Mary Wollstonecraft, like most of the Marys in this chapter, who were all pioneers of a kind, felt passionate about her cause. But it was only really intellectual freedom these petticoteries were fighting for. They were far distant from those women already savouring the sharp, invigorating air of freedom, and perhaps the social and political reformation they dreamed of might have happened more quickly and completely had they been able to look down from the 'Walls of Fame' and notice what certain working women were actually doing.

I think they might have been quite shocked. And, on reflection, not a little envious.

5

UP AND DOING

How much more respectable is the woman who earns her
own bread . . . than the most accomplished beauty!

Mary Wollstonecraft[1]

MARY WOLLSTONECRAFT MUST HAVE REALIZED when she
wistfully wrote the above – which sounds more like a proverb
than an observation – that self-sufficient women, like all society's
female misfits, were traditionally supposed to be ugly – too ugly
to 'earn a living' more conventionally by marrying. There are
plenty of examples: strapping Cutpurse Moll and Sarah Mapp;
journalist Eliza Haywood, whom Alexander Pope so unkindly
described as 'Yon Juno of majestic size, With cow-like udders and
with ox-like eyes;'[2] the exquisitely skilful painter Sarah Biffin,[3]
born without limbs and only three feet tall, or even Mary Astell,
by her own admission 'one to whom nature has not been over
liberal'.[4]

Miss Wollstonecraft should have taken heart, however. She
was writing at a time (in 1792) when less tortured souls
than hers were beginning to discover the satisfaction of a
respectable and successful working life, a life oblivious to

the putative reforms of the Bluestockings and their ilk, requiring no deformity of body or morals, no structured training, nor even, necessarily, any formal education at all, just an uncomplicated spirit of determination and perseverance, and the self-confidence to commit to a career without precedent (or what *we* would recognize as a career, anyway; then, they were just called 'honourable livelihoods').[5]

A career in the forces has always been considered an honourable livelihood. No doubt Christian Cavanagh and Hannah Snell thought it so, along with a small regiment of like-minded military women, when they variously enlisted into the Dragoons, the Marines, the Infantry and the Navy. Most drew pensions on retirement from a grateful state.

None of these adventurers embarked on their careers as women, of course. Their self-confidence did not stretch quite that far. Not content with being camp-followers or sutlers (suppliers of goods and victuals), which were the only openings for undisguised members of their sex in the forces, they chose to mortgage their femininity for the sake of action.[6] When discovery came, as inevitably it did sooner or later, their stories became sensationally popular. These fine 'British Amazons'' exploits were celebrated (and embroidered) in the street literature and ballads of the day, and lustily re-enacted in shows and plays around the country, sometimes starring the heroines themselves, dressed as they used to be when they were men.

Christian Cavanagh (1667–1739) was the first of them to join up. According to her 'autobiography', somewhat over-imaginatively ghost-written in 1740,[7] she lived comfortably enough in her native Dublin, managing a pub her aunt had left her, wed to one of her waiters, Richard Welsh, and the mother of three children. But in about 1692, after four years of marriage, her husband mysteriously disappeared and was not heard of again until a scribbled letter arrived twelve months later, explaining that he had been 'forced' to join the army, and was fighting the French in Flanders.

Christian's reaction seems to have been fuelled more by restlessness and resentment than love or loyalty. She immediately packed off the two surviving children, one to her mother and one to a nurse, and presented herself to Captain Tichborne's Regiment of Foot, bound for Willemstad in the Netherlands, swearing to root out her husband and drag him home to his domestic duty.

The venture needed some careful preparation on her part:

> I cut off my Hair, and dressed me in a Sute of my Husband's, having had the Precaution to quilt the Waistcoat, to preserve my Breasts from hurt, which were not large enough to betray my Sex, and putting on the Wig and Hat I had prepared, I went out and bought me a silver hilted Sword and some Holland shirts . . .[8]

Astonishingly, it was a disguise which served her for some twelve years.[9]

Christian arrived safely in Flanders, and was swept into the Duke of Marlborough's action against the French, being wounded several times, taken prisoner, ransomed, transferred to the Scots Greys (the Second Dragoons), and generally distinguishing herself on the field. In fact, so involved was she in her new career that it was not until 1702 – nearly a decade after she had first set out – that her husband 'occurred to Memory . . . I made what Enquiry I could after him, but in vain; wherefore, I endeavoured, as I concluded him forever lost, to forget him'.[10] Fate is a fickle jade, though, and soon afterwards she spotted the renegade Welsh drinking with, and energetically fondling, a Dutch woman.

Words were exchanged, and a bargain was struck, which required Welsh to remain celibate until the war was over and

Christian could leave the Dragoons. Then they would travel back to Dublin (where she had recently been on leave, to check all was well) and start again – if Christian survived the war.

She was spared, but only just. Her skull was fractured by a shell at Ramillies in 1706, and during subsequent surgery her secret was revealed, and she was dismissed from the queen's service. Admiring officers offered to keep her with them as a cook, and for a while she was glad to stay, as long as she was allowed to pitch her tent at the front of the camp with the soldiers, rather than at the back with the mere women and other hangers-on. She decided to take Welsh back, and conceived another child before Welsh himself was killed at Malplaquet in 1709. Within weeks Christian had married again, but was quickly widowed for a second time, and after two years' (remarkably cheerful) 'maroding', or profitably picking over the bodies and property of the dead enemy, she sailed home to resume the pub, the children and the single life she had left so many years before.

In the meantime one of her children had died; the other had been put in the workhouse by the (unpaid) nurse; and the pub had been seized in her absence. It was a sorry home-coming, and for the rest of Christian's life – spent married to yet another weak and wasteful soldier – she pined for the 'sharp, invigorating air' of the battlefield. She was awarded a pension by Queen Anne in recognition of the wounds she had sustained for her country, and was buried at the age of seventy-two in the Chelsea Pensioners' ground in London with a volley of guns to salute her.

Christian had a number of aliases. Kit Cavanagh is perhaps the best known, but she is catalogued in various libraries as Christian Davies (her final husband's surname) and, more puzzlingly, as 'Mother Ross', apparently after an officer who took her under his wing on witnessing her distress at Welsh's death. But whatever she is called, she remains one of the most colourful characters in the annals of the modern Amazon.

Another such character was Hannah Snell (1723–92), whose

portrait hangs proudly in the Museum of the Royal Marines at Portsmouth. A recent scholar has tried to verify Hannah's life-story,[11] cross-checking dates, places, names, events, and so on. They do not always tally with external evidence, which is not surprising: Hannah was illiterate, caught up in a whirlwind of unwonted action and danger, and well aware (when her fighting career was over, and a new living had to be earned) that a good story courted not only attention, but money. So she told that story – in a book dictated by her in 1750 and sold with a sworn affidavit of veracity – as beguilingly as she could. There was quite enough substance in it for Charles Dickens to include her in an article on 'British Amazons' in his periodical *All the Year Round*,[12] and more than enough for me.[13]

The book's title says it all, really (and it is possibly the longest title ever, so hold tight):

THE FEMALE SOLDIER

or

the Surprising Life and Adventures

of

HANNAH SNELL

Born in the City of Worcester

Who took upon herself the name of James Grey; and, being deserted by her husband, put on men's apparel, and travelled to Coventry in quest of him, where she enlisted in Colonel Guise's Regiment of Foot, and marched with that regiment to Carlisle in the time of the rebellion in Scotland, showing what happened to her in that city, and her desertion from that regiment.

Also

A full and true account of her enlisting afterwards into

[101]

Fraser's Regiment of Marines, then at Portsmouth, and her being drafted out of that regiment and sent on board the *Swallow* sloop-of-war, one of Admiral Boscawen's squadron then bound for the East Indies. With the many vicissitudes of fortune she met with during that expedition, particularly at the siege of Pondicherry, where she received twelve wounds; likewise the surprising accident by which she came to hear of the death of her faithless husband, whom she went in quest of.

The whole containing

The most surprising incidents that have happened in any preceding age [!], wherein is laid open all her adventures, in men's clothes, for near five years without her sex ever being discovered.[14]

Details of Hannah's early life are a little hazy: she seems to have assumed her brother-in-law's identity when abandoned (like Christian) by her husband, a Dutch sailor by the name of Summs. She did not search for him over-zealously, though, and must have been one of those potent and spirited women waiting only for a respectable excuse to let themselves loose on a male world. After she left the Marines in 1750, of her own volition and with a healthy pension, together with 'the liberty of wearing Men's Cloaths and also a Cockade in her hat',[15] she became an accomplished self-publicist, producing her best-seller and touring with a stage show in which she featured dressed in 'Regimentals' and performing a series of artillery exercises and songs (bordering on the bawdy). The crowds loved her.

Annoyingly, the novelty soon wore off, and by 1760 she had settled with her second husband in Wapping, running a pub called The Widow in Masquerade or, more popularly, The Female Warrior. The business failed, and she retired to a tediously quiet life near Norwich with husband number three.

After the onset of severe mental illness, Hannah died, sadly, in a cell at the Bethlehem Hospital for the insane – London's notorious 'Bedlam' – and even though she was buried, like Christian, at Chelsea, her grave was unmarked. I like to remember her in the words of a song she inspired, published at the height of her fame in 1750. It is suitably lusty:

> Hannah in Briggs [breeches] behav'd so well,
> That none her softer sex could tell:
> Nor was her Policy confounded,
> When near the Mark of Nature wounded:
> Which proves, what Men will scarce admit,
> That Women are for Secrets fit.
>
> That healthful Blood cou'd keep so long
> Amidst young fellows hale and strong,
> Demonstrates, tho' a seeming Wonder,
> That Love to Courage truckles under.
>
> O how her Bed mate bit his Lips,
> And mark'd the Spreading of her Hips;
> And curs'd the Blindness of his Youth,
> When she confess'd the Naked Truth!
> Her Fortitude, to no man's second,
> To Woman's Honour must be reckon'd ...
>
> 'Twas thought Achilles' greatest Glory,
> That Homer rose to sing his Story;
> And Alexander mourn'd his Lot,
> That no such Bard cou'd then be got, –
> But Hannah's praise no Homer needs;
> She lives to sing her Proper Deeds.[16]

There are plenty of other histories of women who, like Christian and Hannah, lived as men amongst men to earn their bread. 'William Brown' (born *c*.1783) was a black sailor from Edinburgh, and was only discovered to be a woman in 1815 when paid off (with the rest of the crew) after eleven years' service aboard the 110-gun *Queen Charlotte*. For part of that time, fighting in the Napoleonic wars, she had been 'captain of the foretop', in charge of all the men who worked the sails way up at the top of the masts. According to a report in the *Annual Register* of 1815, she exhibited 'all the traits of a British tar' and took her grog amongst her late messmates 'with the greatest gaiety'.[17] Even after declaring her sex, she was welcomed back aboard the ship on its next commission as a volunteer, and went on to serve in another ship, the *Bombay*, for which no muster records survive. At that point she fades from history.

A somewhat similar account to Hannah's vigorous life-story was published in 1809, telling the picaresque tale of Mary Anne Talbot (1778–1808), born the illegitimate child (allegedly one of about sixteen) of Lord William Talbot, Steward to the Household of George III. From the age of five until she was fourteen Mary lived in a bleak boarding-school, her mother having died in childbirth; her guardian then entrusted her to a friend of his, one Captain Essex Bowen, who, having taken a violent fancy to her, decided to take her with him on his posting to Santa Domingo disguised as 'John Taylor', his servant. There followed a series of adventures in successive incarnations as drummer-boy, cabin-boy and powder-monkey. Mary's career encompassed capture (by 'William Brown's' ship, the *Queen Charlotte*, on one occasion, while Mary was serving as a mercenary on a French vessel), imprisonment in both France and London, and at last pensioned retirement as a wounded serviceman (or woman) of regrettably slender means.

Once out of the service, Mary declined fast, and did not even benefit from the sales of her story ('Related by Herself'): she was only thirty when she died the year before it was published,[18] and I must admit that it is hard to authenticate what may well be an over-fanciful account. That does not, however, mean that Mary was not a highly enterprising character: whether in battle or in business, she obviously tried her best to prosper.

Yet another British Amazon, Phoebe Hessel (1713?–1821), was well over a hundred by the time *she* expired, and her gravestone in Brighton (paid for by the local pawnbroker) hardly does her life justice, recording only that it was erected:

In Memory of
PHOEBE HESSEL
who was born at Stepney in the Year 1713.
She served for many Years
as a private soldier in the 5th Reg. of foot
in different parts of Europe
and in the year 1745 fought under the command
of the DUKE of CUMBERLAND
at the Battle of Fontenoy
where she received a Bayonet wound in her Arm.
Her long life which commenced in the time of
QUEEN ANNE
extended to the reign of
GEORGE IV
by whose munificence she received comfort
and support in her latter Years
She died at Brighton where she had long resided
December 12th 1821 Aged 108 Years.

Phoebe supplemented the pension paid her by George IV (who apparently thought her a particularly 'jolly old fellow')[19] by toddling around the villages of West Sussex with a donkey, selling wet fish, and then, as her strength diminished in her ninth decade, by peddling those boiled sweets called bulls'-eyes, fruit and pin-cushions from a stall at the bottom of Brighton's Marine Parade, and telling rambling stories of her adventurous

[105]

youth. 'Other people die, but I cannot,' she used to complain (or boast): she had too much still to do.

The already well-documented phenomenon, strangely prevalent during the eighteenth century, of females finding physical, emotional, even sexual freedom by impersonating men is a fascinating one. Christian, Hannah and the others excelled in near-impossible circumstances during their working lives in the forces: their resilient strength of character was extraordinary. The *Dictionary of National Biography*, discussing Christian Cavanagh at the end of the nineteenth century, rather acerbically put her success as a soldier down to the fact that she had obviously become coarse and 'unsexed' in the army, and was therefore no longer a true woman at all. (She probably wasn't very pretty, either.)

Changing oneself into a man, however temporarily, was not the only way for a woman to forge an ostensibly respectable career. She might capitalize, instead, on the ultra-feminine accomplishments of the arts, turning what had been treated as an acceptable but passive pastime for those who could afford it into a lucrative business. I mentioned Sarah Biffin at the beginning of this chapter: she was successful not only because she was a curiosity, painting with her mouth and, being tiny herself, choosing to produce miniature paintings; her work sold because of its intrinsic beauty and finesse, and she became one of a band of professional ladies happy to use their artistic training and skills for profit.

In the applied arts, Hester Bateman (*c.*1709–94) excelled as one of the age's finest domestic and ecclesiastical silversmiths. She was illiterate, the mother of five children, and the widow (by 1760) of a gold-chain-maker; she became the proprietor of a company producing graceful and high-quality silver (which stayed in the family until the mid nineteenth century), the proud possessor of her own hallmark, and acknowledged 'Queen of English Silversmiths'.[20]

[106]

Eliza Fay (1756–1815) was somewhat less successful, although just as imaginative in her career as Hester. Eliza was a travelling saleswoman. She sourced muslins in India, and exported them to North America aboard her own good ship, the *Minerva*. Or that was the plan, anyway. In fact, Eliza started out as a mantua-maker (mantuas were silk gowns): it was an occupation she turned to when she left her adulterous husband in 1780 while they were resident in India. Anthony Fay was a lowly advocate in the Civil Service; his wife was an energetic, enthusiastic, but unrealistic businesswoman, determined to succeed without him.

Mantua-making did not pay enough for Eliza, so she tried a little speculation, buying a share in the *Minerva*, only for the vessel to be scuttled soon afterwards when a bottle of aquafortis, or nitric acid, exploded on board and set the decks on fire. After some hasty repairs it was made seaworthy again, and Eliza sailed back to India in 1796 to investigate the muslin trade. Her first consignment of cloth, bound from Calcutta to America, was spoiled when the waters of the Hooghly river leached into the *Minerva*'s leaky hold, and the cloth was virtually unsaleable by the time it reached New York.

Unbeaten, Eliza wrote an account of her life which was no doubt designed to raise the money, probably by subscription, to clear her mounting debts. But only a year later she died in Calcutta, her sole possessions – two pianos, a gold watch, a wig, and a book entitled *Remarks on Establishing an Institution for the Support and Education of Unfortunate Females* – revealing a quixotic optimism to the last.[21] Her book was eventually published by her creditors in 1817, part autobiography, part travel account, but it was not a great success.

Travel-writing was a field particularly attractive to more educated women than Biffin, Bateman or Fay, seeking an apparently genteel as well as honourable livelihood – although in practice, it was an exhausting way to make a living. Like sketching and making elegant music, journal-keeping was a *sine qua non* of a polite young lady's upbringing; several enterprising authors extended that art to provide the reading (and travelling) public with an increasingly valuable service.

Louisa Costello (1799–1870) was the first professional woman travel-writer of all (closely followed by the Austrian, Ida Pfeiffer), having first tried to keep the wolf from her impoverished family's door by working as an artist in Paris. She then became a copyist of illuminated manuscripts – reminiscent of Christine de Pizan – before publishing her first travelogue, *A Summer amongst the Bocages and the Vines*, in 1840. More books followed, on France, Austria and Italy, each prettily suggesting itineraries and excursions, and with plenty of historical and artistic embroidery.[22]

Louisa hit the market, as it were, at exactly the right time. A certain Mr Thomas Cook had founded a travel business in 1841; growing affluence and opportunity meant that more people were visiting the Continent than ever before, and it was heartily recommended that no true tourist should venture there without copies of 'Miss Costello' and 'Miss Starke' in their carpet-bag. For if Louisa provided the background, the practical details of tourism were filled in by the earliest comprehensive guide-books to Europe ever written, produced not by John Murray, nor even by Herr Baedeker, but by an assiduous English spinster, Mariana Starke.

Mariana (1762?–1838) was a pioneer of independent travel, or travel for those, as she put it, 'who may not choose to incur the Expence attendant upon travelling with a Courier.'[23] She made it her business to cover the whole of Europe, from France to Hungary, Russia to Spain (and all points in between), noting down places to stay, places to visit, the distances between them, what to take abroad, what to seek out or guard against, and how much everything would cost. Her *Travels on the Continent* ran into tens of editions, and set a basic pattern for guide-books valid ever since.

Louisa Costello needed her royalties from these travel books, amongst several other literary works, to live and to finance the next of her journeys; Miss Starke, on the other hand, probably had private money at the start of her writing career (she was daughter of the Governor of Madras . . .). But the receipts on all the reissues of *Travels on the Continent* must have been quite considerable. Between them, these two British women inspired many a Victorian lady to set out on her own voyage of discovery into a world a little more familiar, and therefore less threatening, than before.

I should not think Mary Seacole (1805–81) worried too much about precedent, though, when she set sail from her native Jamaica towards Europe in the 1850s. In Mary (unlike poor Eliza Fay) the spirit of achievement flourished abundantly, and fuelled everything she did: 'All my life long I . . . followed the impulse which led me to be up and doing,' she states in her rousing autobiography, *Wonderful Adventures of Mrs Seacole in Many Lands*.[24] Mary's mother was a freed African slave, a 'doctress' or healer in Kingston, who was married to a Scottish army officer with whom she kept a hotel for members of the British garrison stationed in Jamaica. When Mary was twelve she was given the opportunity to sail to Britain, where she stayed with some relations for a year. She realized she was different from her fair-skinned cousins, but thought that was only because she nurtured an unfeminine appetite for adventure and it did not worry her.

This first voyage sparked off Mary's lifelong desire to explore the world, and her place in it. When she next visited England, it was as a traveller in pickles and preserves, recipes she had learned from her mother, made herself and successfully exported. The profits, along with the small legacy her husband Horatio Seacole left her, were put into a 'personal travelling fund', while she subsisted on the proceeds of the hotel (which she ran after her mother's death), and on the practice of her inherited skills as a nurse. She sailed to the Bahamas to collect shells to sell back in Jamaica; she went across to Panama to set up another hotel on the isthmus, bustling with prospective gold-diggers on their way to California; she opened a shop selling homemade clothes, pots of guava jelly, and more of her pickles. And in 1854, when news of the outbreak of war filtered west from the Crimea, she realized her most ambitious enterprise yet by sailing back to Britain and applying to join Florence Nightingale at the front as a nurse.

Memories of the suspicion with which her cousins had treated her came flooding back to Mary when first the War Office and then Miss Nightingale's outfit in London (composed mostly of medically inexperienced upper-class ladies) declined even to interview her. But she refused to be daunted, and with staggering acuity found herself a business partner willing to underwrite with her the establishment of another hotel, this time at Balaclava.

The British Hotel duly opened, run by 'Mother Seacole', and became renowned for its warm welcome, comparatively comfortable lodging, its good food (admired by none other than the celebrated French chef, Alexis Soyer), and its homely atmosphere. Mary continued to diversify, even here: she nursed all those who came to her for help – Briton, Turk or Russian – and went out on to the front-line herself, hauling a vast sack laden with everything from sponge cakes and field dressings to tooth-powder and socks. She enjoyed herself in the Crimea 'amazingly', she said, and so appreciative of her care and compassion were her patients and patrons that a pension was raised, on her return to England at the end of the war, to keep her exhausted body (but indomitable soul) in some kind of comfort.

Mary died in London, and her grave, tended and honoured by the Jamaican Nurses' Association, records her medical service in the West Indies, Panama and the Crimea. She was a gifted nurse, to be sure, but a woman of enterprise and a keen adventurer too.

An 'unprotected female', as she gladly put it, in charge of herself
and her life.

Keenness and passion are essential to the women of enterprise;
drive, I suppose we would call it now, a commitment to one's
work, and the mental and physical energy to flourish. Vigour was
not a quality upper-class ladies were expected to revel in, though,
unless it be the sort of amateur ardency the Duchess of Newcastle,
Anne Conway and those other *femmes savantes* enjoyed in the
seventeenth century. Enthusiasm like that of Christian Cavanagh,
Eliza Fay, or Mary Seacole smacked (at first) of vulgarity, and
even writers like Costello and Starke could be slightly disparag-
ingly classed as (literally) journeywomen, albeit superior ones,
until it was remembered that these were not well-bred women,
not true ladies: they were not entitled to respect, but bought it
instead. By the same token, so little was expected of them as poor
and/or uneducated women, that, as Samuel Johnson observed of
women preachers, 'Like a dog's walking on his hinder legs [i]t
is not done well; but you are surprised to find it done at all.'

The first working women to break through unequivocally to
intellectual pre-eminence and fame were the palaeobotanist Mary
Anning and her contemporary, the astronomer Caroline Herschel.
In their careers they combined an honourable livelihood with
acknowledged expertise (acknowledged, that is, by men who
knew . . .), even though yet again, neither had benefited from
anything but the scantest schooling.

There is a shop in the Dorset coastal town of Lyme Regis called
The Fossil Shop. It is a direct descendant of an eighteenth-century
wooden table that used to be set out by the shoreline, groaning
with all sorts of geological curiosities for sale. These ammonites
and belemnites and assorted bones and corals had been found
by a local carpenter, Richard Anning, who used to take his wife
Molly, their son Joseph and daughter Mary scavenging under
the perilous cliffs of Lyme for fossils. Mary (1799–1847) was

the most accomplished 'fossilizer' of them all, still remembered by generations of British children in that tongue-twisting song:

> She sells sea-shells on the sea-shore,
> The shells she sells are sea-shells, I'm sure,
> For if she sells sea-shells on the sea-shore,
> Then I'm sure she sells sea-shore shells.[25]

As time went on Mary graduated from the stall by the beach to 'a little dirty shop', according to one visitor in 1732, 'with hundreds of specimens piled around, and in the greatest disorder. She [was] the presiding Deity, a prim, pedantic vinegar looking, thin female, shrewd and rather satirical in her conversation.'[26] She had graduated, too, from a Dorset pauper to a distinguished pensioner of the Geological Society in London, who knew more about the infant science of palaeontology 'than anyone else in the kingdom'.[27]

Mary's life was a hard and in many ways an unhappy one. Her father, Richard, died when she was eleven from tuberculosis and complications following a fall while out fossilizing under Lyme's notorious overhanging headland, Black Ven. Towards the end of his life he was unable to work, and what with extra medical expenses the family was left £120 in debt at his death. His wife Molly tried to earn an income by taking Joseph and Mary away from the local Dissenters' school they had been attending and putting them to fossil-hunting full-time, but the Annings could only sell (to local collectors, mostly) what they found, and if they found nothing special, they went hungry.

It was a simple problem to Mary: she must expose better fossils than before, and learn how to assemble, preserve and present them as marketable to specialists. The year 1812 was a good one: between them Joseph and Mary unearthed what later became identified as an Ichthyosaur, and sold it for £23. It was a fabulous skeleton of a fishy sort of crocodile, extracted and pieced together with instinctive skill and meticulousness by Mary, and displayed to this day in the British Museum of Natural History. There were only slim pickings for several years after the Ichthyosaur's discovery, though, and the family subsisted on parish relief for at least the next three years. By 1820 they had reached near desperation, and were brought back from the brink by Gideon Mantell, an admiring and sympathetic geologist who auctioned part of his own fossil collection

> . . . for the benefit of the poor woman [Molly Anning] and her son and daughter at Lyme who have in truth found almost all the fine things [in the collection] which have been submitted to scientific investigation: when I went to Charmouth and Lyme last summer I found these people in considerable difficulty – in the act of selling their furniture to pay their rent – in consequence of their not having found one good fossil for a twelve month.[28]

It was a parlous profession. But now that Mary's skills and credibility had been endorsed by a gentleman scholar, her influence, and confidence, began to swell. Drawn to Lyme by its abundantly fruitful cliffs, professional scientists and amateurs alike would consult both her shop and her expertise, learning from her example how to identify specimens from a mere handful of bones, how to coax whole skeletons from their crumbling beds, and how to record and arrange them – chronologically as well as physically – into the blueprints of all those creatures supposed (by the more enlightened) to be the inhabitants of the earth before Noah's flood.

Mary grew to resent the avaricious spirit in which her knowledge was sometimes received. She complained that her finds were rarely acknowledged (museums preferring to credit

[113]

those who donated exhibits rather than those who discovered or sold them), telling one of her patrons that the world had used her ill:

> [A]ccording to her account these men of learning have sucked her brains, and made a great deal by publishing works, of which she furnished the contents, while she derived none of the advantages . . .[29]

Maybe that was why the visitor to her shop in 1782 had found such a bitter proprietor. She was proud of her accomplishment, as the untutored daughter of an artisan, in becoming such an authority in the field, and thought she deserved more acclaim – and reward – than she received. I hope she was mollified when the Prime Minister, Lord Melbourne, and the joint worthies of the British Association for the Advancement of Science in Dublin and the Geological Society of London awarded her an annuity during the years of her debilitating decline with breast cancer. When the King of Saxony visited Lyme in 1844, and came, naturally, to consult Mary, she happily signed her autograph for a member of his party with the proud declaration that she, like the King, was 'well known throughout the whole of Europe'. She certainly deserved to be.

Modern scientists have catalogued Mary's pioneering finds with admiration: the plesiosaur she discovered in 1823 (priced at £100); the first British example of a pterodactyl in 1828; a wonderfully complex fish, the squaloraja, in 1829, and another even finer plesiosaur a year later (this time sold for 200 guineas). They have noted her correspondence with other palaeontologists of the day, and the references to her (usually, it has to be said, in small footnotes) in scholarly geological publications. The natural historian Sir Crispin Tickell, Mary's great-great-great-nephew, sums up the spirit of her life and work best, I think, when he writes of her as 'an independent-minded person of great intelligence':

> ... no dainty heroine from children's tales, no conventional creature of fantasy, no mere local prodigy, no defender of women's rights, no prettified hand maiden of science ... [but] tough, practical, complex, generous, sometimes prickly ... who surmounted the obstacles of her sex and circumstances to help lay the foundations of a new science of the earth.[30]

Caroline Herschel, a scientist not of the earth but of the heavens, was already forty-nine when Mary was born, and yet Caroline outlived Mary, lasting, phenomenally, until the age of ninety-seven. The Herschel family came from Hanover, Caroline's father Isaac being an oboist in a Prussian Army band, and those few children, of a brood of ten, who survived long enough, were sent to the local garrison school. Caroline left when she was fourteen. Both she and her father were keen on furthering her education – she was obviously a bright and thoughtful child – but her mother disapproved on principle of learned women, and trained Caroline instead in knitting and needlework, sending her to a seamstress to learn how to earn a proper living. Desperately inept at sewing, Caroline meanwhile managed to acquire a little French, to snatch the odd violin lesson from her father (when mother wasn't listening), and to practise singing, which she loved to do above all else.

Isaac Herschel died when Caroline was seventeen, and with him she lost her greatest ally in the struggle to avoid a future in domestic service, until, that is, her brother William sent for her in 1772 to join him in Bath, where he was working as a musician. He needed a housekeeper, and despite the fact that she could speak no English, and would no doubt gravely disappoint her mother, Caroline accepted his invitation. She felt there was no choice:

> I saw that all my executions [as a very bad seamstress] would not save me from becoming a burden to my brothers; and I had by this time imbibed too much pride for submitting to take a place as a ladiesmaid, and for a Governess I was not qualified for want of knowledge in languages. And I never forgot the caution my dear father gave me against all thoughts of marrying, saying as I was neither hansom [sic] nor rich [and only 4′ 3″ tall . . .] it was not likely that anyone would make me an offer, till perhaps, when far advanced in life, some old man might take me for my good qualities . . .'[31]

William's particular passion, apart from music, was astronomy. When he met Caroline in London after her long journey from Hanover, he took her to see the sights, which turned out to involve a tour of all the opticians' shops he could find, so that he could ogle the lovely lenses. Caroline was bewildered.

In Bath, she took lessons from William in English, music and mathematics every morning, in return for keeping her brother's house and increasingly helping with his astronomical hobby. For a while she trained – and performed – as an oratorio singer, but refused to share the stage with any conductor other than her brother, and as he became more and more embroiled in the stars (especially on his appointment as Court Astronomer in 1782, and subsequent marriage), Caroline's singing career came to an end. Eventually she became William's amanuensis, not only in the mundane matters of spooning food into his mouth while he sat at the telescope on clear nights, or grinding and polishing the many mirrors necessary for observations (some measuring ten feet across), but recording those observations, helping to construct the telescopes William made for sale, and 'sweeping the heavens' herself for recalcitrant stars hiding in the corners.

Gradually, Caroline assumed greater responsibility: she corresponded with William's astronomical colleagues and minded the stars for him when he was away; she started cataloguing his observations and publishing them, and then moved on to her own observations and interests (which she indulged only when all of William's work had been done, of course). She became respected in her own right as a thorough and able scientist, whom the Astronomer Royal, Nevil Maskelyne, was proud to call 'my worthy sister in astronomy'.

By 1786 the Herschels were living in Datchet, near Windsor. Their garden was planted with elephantine telescopes, and Caroline spent night after night frowning at the constellations. There is a delightful entry in her diary for 1 August:

> I have calculated 100 nebulae to-day, and this evening I saw an object which I believe will prove to-morrow night to be a comet.
>
> Aug. 2. To-day I calculated 150 nebulae. I fear it will not be clear tonight, it has been raining throughout the whole day, but seems now to clear up a little.
>
> 1 o'clock; the object of last night *is a Comet*.[32]

The discovery of this, dubbed by Fanny Burney 'the first lady's comet', bought Caroline much personal kudos. So did the publication by the Royal Society in 1798 of a catalogue and an index of stars,[33] and the appearance of *The Reduction and Arrangement in the Form of a Catalogue in Zones of all the Star Clusters and Nebulae observed by Sir William Herschel in his Sweeps*. The latter won her the Royal Astronomical Society's Gold Medal in 1828, and honorary membership a year later.

Caroline loved her life with William. It was not easy, however; her work was physically dangerous as well as mentally absorbing:

> That my fears of danger and accidents were not wholly imaginary, I had an unlucky proof on the night of the 31st December. The evening had been cloudy, but about ten o'clock a few stars became visible, and in the greatest hurry all was got ready for observing. My brother, at the front of the telescope, directed me to make some alteration in the lateral motion, which was done by machinery ... At each end of the machine ... was an iron hook, such as butchers use for hanging their joints upon, and having to run in the dark on ground covered a foot deep with melting snow, I fell on one of these hooks, which entered my right leg above the knee. My brother's call "Make haste!" I could only answer by a pitiful cry, "I am hooked!" He and the workmen were instantly with me, but they could not lift me without leaving nearly two ounces of my flesh behind ...
>
> I had, however, the comfort to know that my brother was no loser through this accident, for the remainder of the night was cloudy ...[34]

For all the plaudits and all the fulfilment she found in being a practical scientist (hazards notwithstanding), there was one thing that gratified Caroline about her work more than any other. As William's assistant, she was *paid wages* by the Crown of £50 a year. So she was not a burden on anyone else, as she had once feared; she was up and doing, working hard and being useful as her mother had always urged her to be; she was respected not for her looks but, as Wollstonecraft put it, for the honour and skill with which she 'earned her bread'. And that bread tasted sweet:

[I]n October [1787] I received £12/10/-, being the first quarterly payment of my salary; and the first money in all my lifetime I ever thought myself at liberty to spend *to my own liking.*[35]

6

UNGENTLEWOMEN

[T]here was too much of her to be held within the prescribed
and safe limits allotted to woman . . .

Lola Montez[1]

WHEN I FIRST STARTED RESEARCHING this book, and explaining
what it was going to be about to friends, I met with two common
responses: either it was assumed that the book would be about
rebels, or about pioneers. In reality, the two are hardly mutually
exclusive; what they meant was that whatever these women did
by way of a career would be motivated either by a bloody-minded
need to be different, or an evangelical urge to advance. Education
was the key, without which no woman could hope to succeed in
developing a decent independent living, and all who did succeed
would surely be only too pleased to have illuminated the way a
little for those of their sisters with the gumption to follow in their
footsteps.

I did not have the courage to tell these friends that I wasn't
confining myself to those earning a *decent* independent living,
or that it was generally the uneducated who shone the brightest,
and the selfish who prospered the best. Many of the individuals

I was uncovering did not give a damn about inspiring others, or even, strangely, about breaking down political barriers. They just responded to circumstances and capitalized on their own high spirits and strength of character. They were not being noble pioneers at all.

But bloody-minded rebels? Judge for yourself. There are certainly a few in Chapter 3, 'Madde Pranckes and Merry Molls', reacting against the limitations of social and/or moral propriety; the 'Petticoteries' were full of women whose words, rather than deeds, showed their discontent with the received wisdom of their (mostly male) peers. But I would still maintain that most of the women we have met so far did what they did because they needed the money, recognized potential in themselves, and then worked to realize it in ways that were contrary to the expectations of their contemporaries. Many were not aware of historical trends, so can hardly have been making a political point. They may not even have surprised themselves in their careers. It is only we commentators who are shocked, because we believe what has been written about working women in general, instead of witnessing what they did as individuals.

In this chapter, I am going to look at rebellion, in all its forms. For the ungentlewomen included, an honourable livelihood was not enough, nor were they satisfied with defying their sex by choosing highly unfeminine careers. They craved some extra excitement – the stimulation of travelling, of changing places or identities. They sought not only new lives, but new worlds, because their own were simply not quite large enough.

And where better to seek a new life but in the land of liberty? Apart from the seventeenth-century colonial settlers, turning their heads and hands to whatever needed doing from newspaper-printing to auctioneering, or gunsmithing to jailkeeping,[2] and the subsequent homesteaders and pioneers who forged the future, there is little documented history of individual, independent working women in America before the Declaration of Independence. Not until the nineteenth century do we really begin to see Americans flourishing in occupations away from those which were or have since become traditionally associated with women. The plantation managers like Mrs Bowling, described in 1782 as 'one of the greatest land-owners in Virginia, and proprietor of half the town of Petersburg,'[3] or Eliza Pinckney, who farmed estates producing indigo and silk of rare quality,[4] would be exceptions. And there were philanthropists and educationalists aplenty, but they were not usually working for a living, honourable or otherwise.

I am not concerned with the many American lady-professionals who burgeoned during the mid to late 1800s (by 'lady-professionals' I mean those women like Maria Mitchell, the first lady-professor, or Lucy Hobbs, the first lady-dentist, or Louise Blanchard Bethune, the first lady-architect); they have books to themselves in any case. Unhampered by generations of home-grown misogyny, and leavened by the republican ideal, educated white American women assumed the right at least to venture at equality with men (they were even allowed to vote, in certain states and with certain prohibitions, as early as 1776).[5] Equality did not necessarily mean parity, though: for the Americans I'm referring to, it meant earning the right to be what one of them called a 'self-sustaining woman',[6] and supporting oneself, and perhaps others, as a man did. They were outrageous not necessarily for wanting a career in the first place, but for choosing such wild and wayward ones.

Anne Newport Royall (1769–1854) is a good example. This is what the ex-President of the United States, John Quincy Adams, had to say of her in 1844:

> Stripped of her sex's delicacy, but unable to forfeit its privilege of gentle treatment from the other, she goes about like a virago-errant in enchanted armour, redeeming herself from the cramps of indigence by the notoriety of her eccentricities.[7]

[123]

Maybe his odium was well-founded. Mrs Royall certainly never found a use for charm. She had tried that when petitioning the powers-that-be in Washington and her home state of Virginia for a share in her husband's estate (slave-owner General Royall had been a hero of the revolution, but had failed to provide satisfactorily for his widow). It did not work. And so, at the unlovely age of fifty-four, she began trying to earn her keep. Unable to afford a home of her own, she travelled from Baltimore to Connecticut, by way of New York, scribbling down descriptions of the people she saw as she went, and in 1826 *Sketches of History, Life, and Manners in the United States* was published, underwritten by her late husband's fellow freemasons (to whom Mrs Royall appealed in her hour of need), and damned by those it ridiculed as libellous and tawdry.

Mrs Royall's writing was journalistic in style, and uncompromising. She interviewed various characters encountered during seven years' pretty continuous travelling throughout the southern and eastern states between 1824 and 1831, and used to specialize in uncovering the unsound. She would spit, in print (perhaps not only in print), at 'Holy Willies' or 'Hallelujah Holdforths': these were Presbyterians, one of whose leaders she addressed succinctly as 'a damned old bald-headed son of a bitch'. Jews she approved, though, along with Catholics, all Germans and, naturally, freemasons.

Ten acidic collections of these interviews and peregrinations appeared altogether, along with one execrable novel. Royall claimed that none brought her a profit. 'Of all the works I have published,' she complained, 'I have not been able from sales to pay for the paper, much less the printing . . .'[8] Booksellers were to blame: they were all cheats, and so probably Presbyterians. Her scanty diet on the road consisted of coffee for breakfast and tea for dinner, and her feet bled through the shredded leather of her boots as she trudged along trying to earn her bread.

Yet her books *did* sell. Or at least, they were read, and citizens of towns known to be next on the itinerary used to quake at her coming. Occasionally measures would be taken to silence this 'virago errant'. In 1827 she was pushed down some steps so vigorously that her leg snapped and she dislocated an ankle; two years later she became the first woman in America to be charged as a 'common scold'. Much time and money was spent in an attempt to unearth the law that would imprison her (during which time, in court, she furiously penned sketches of the judge and witnesses to publish at a later date), but it was too abstruse a business, and she was released, after having paid a fine for libel.

Mrs Royall finally came to rest in Washington DC in 1831, at the age of sixty-two. Here she devoted her terrifying energy to exacting a pension from Congress in recognition of her husband's wartime prowess, and to issuing a four-page partly political weekly paper called *Paul Pry*, which this time, due to some robust self-restraint, was a success. It ran for five years, attaining national circulation by the end, and was succeeded by an even milder periodical, *The Huntress*, which saw Annie to her grave in 1854, a wily, wiry old woman of eighty-five.

Seven years after Annie Royall's death, the American Civil War broke out. And just as the free-booting years of the eighteenth century fetched out characters like the pirates Bonny and Read, or soldiers and sailors like Cavanagh and Snell in Britain, the Civil War in America offered a whole host of women the chance for a fundamental change of life. There were fighters, to be sure, whose stories play a nicely heroic part in the annals of the United States.[9] I'm interested here, though, in those who went beyond the battlefield, as the Canadian Sarah Edmonds did, and the Cuban, Loreta Janeta Velasquez.

Sarah Edmonds (1842–98) was a serial career woman. She began her working life (having run away from a brutal father in New Brunswick) as a milliner. But that was too tame, and so was everything she considered available to her as a young woman, including marriage to an elderly but enthusiastic local farmer. So, according to her own account,[10] she decided to avenge years of oppression and cancel her femininity to become a man – a good man:

> You have expressed a desire to know what led me to assume male attire. I will try to tell you. I think I was born into this world with some dormant antagonism toward man. I hope I have outgrown it measurably but my infant soul was impressed with a sense of my mother's wrongs before I ever saw the light and I probably drew from her breast with my daily food my love of independence and my hatred of male tyranny.[11]

Besides, Sarah was intoxicated by 'the freedom and glorious independence of masculinity'.[12] This led to stints as a Bible salesman in Connecticut and Michigan, a bookseller's agent in Nova Scotia, and then enlistment in 1861 into the Unionist volunteers as Franklin Thompson.

Ironically, Sarah chose to serve as a male nurse rather than a fighting soldier. Perhaps she felt she had made her point by pretending to be a male and could now exercise the choice denied her before. In any case, she progressed to riding on spying missions behind enemy lines, disguised on one occasion as 'an Irish biddy peddling cakes and comfits from her wicker basket',[13] and on another as a young black cook in a Confederate camp. She was also a valuable aide-de-camp before her desertion from the army with a fellow soldier, her lover, in 1863.

Sarah had now mortgaged her male identity, and went on to marry, to mother children, to run an orphanage, to nurse, and to publish a best-seller with *Nurse and Spy in the Union Army: Comprising the Adventures and Experiences of a Woman in Hospitals, Camps and Battle-Fields* (1865). And like Cavanagh and Snell she was even, despite her desertion, granted an army pension in the end.

I wonder if she ever came across Loreta Janeta Velasquez (born 1842) during her army career. Loreta, an exact contemporary, had joined up in Alabama, and with Sarah's enemies, the Confederates. Assuming a male uniform was not a political matter for Loreta, but a spiritual one. She had always been a passionate girl, born in Havana but educated at a boarding-school in New Orleans. There, she says, she

> expended all pocket money not in candies and cakes, as most girls are in the habit of doing, but in the purchase of books which related the . . . lives of kings, princes, and soldiers. The story of the siege of Orleans, in particular . . . thrilled my young heart and sent my blood bounding through my veins with excitement. Joan of Arc became my heroine, and I longed for an opportunity to become such another she. I was fond of imagining myself as the hero of the most stupendous adventures.[14]

That opportunity presented itself with the outbreak of war. She was nineteen years old in 1861, already four years married and the mother of two children who had both died in their infancy, and *bored*. At first she thought she could fight this war vicariously through her husband William, whom she instructed to enlist as a Confederate. This proved a little tricky for William, who was already a serving Unionist officer, but he obliged. Loreta was not satisfied though, and decided that the only way of engaging properly in this 'stupendous adventure' would be to take part in it herself.

This time her husband was not so indulgent. 'He would not listen to anything I had to say on the subject,' she grumbled, 'and all I could do was await his departure for the seat of war, in order to put my plans into execution without his knowledge. I was obstinately bent on realizing the dream of my life, whether he approved or not.'[15] So within three days of the hapless husband's departure, Loreta commissioned a special uniform, appropriately shaped and padded to conceal her figure; she cut her hair, affixed a fine false moustache, assumed the name of Harry T. Buford, and left for war.

First she went to neighbouring Arkansas to recruit a battalion of men (this career woman did *not* need the money at this stage) – 236 of them commissioned and equipped at her own expense – then she planned to march to her husband's camp, present herself and her men to him, and thus earn both his respect and permission to fight alongside. However, William was killed before she could reach him, whereupon his distraught widow relinquished her command, swapped her men for a few horses, and galloped to the Confederate Army HQ in search of battle. Now she had neither husband nor children to consider, she was free to expend her life in her cause, and was determined to enjoy it, as at the notorious Battle of Bull Run:

> I cannot pretend to express in words what I felt as I found myself one among thousands of combatants, who were about to engage in a deadly and desperate struggle. The supreme moment of my life had arrived . . . As the hot July sun mounted upwards through the almost cloudless sky, and the mists of the morning dispersed . . . the approach of the enemy could be distinctly traced by the clouds of dust raised, and once in a while, the gleam of the bayonets . . . The desultory firing with which the battle opened was soon followed by rapid volleys, and ere the morning was far advanced, the sharp rattling of musketry, the roar of the artillery, and the yelling of the soldiers, developed into an incessant tumult . . . At noon the battle was at its fiercest, and the scene was grand beyond description.[16]

Bull Run was in 1861; by February 1862 the novelty of all that pomp and circumstance had worn off. 'Several times I felt as though I could stand it no longer, and was tempted to give the whole thing up, and lie down upon the ground and die.'[17] Then, two months later, something happened that Loreta had feared more than any battle: she was discovered. She had been extensively wounded by mortar shrapnel and during her treatment her caked and stinking uniform – with its padding – was necessarily removed.

Loreta was still not dismissed from the army. She stayed on in the Intelligence unit, as a spy, until 1864. Sometimes she posed as an itinerant cake-seller, or a cartridge-packer in an arsenal; once she wheedled her way into the enemy's confidence as 'a widow-woman in greatly reduced circumstances', which by now must have been somewhat close to the bone.

Loreta's book *The Woman in Battle, A Narrative of the Exploits, Adventures, and Travels of Madame Loreta Janeta Velasquez . . .* (1876) is disappointingly terse about what happened after the war. Apparently she tried a spot of blockade-running right at the end of hostilities before making 'a couple of interesting tours in Europe' and another in South America. She married a further three times, had four more children, worked briefly as a 'Bounty and Substitute Broker' in New York (probably for the military), and then 'went in for mining on the Pacific Slope' (probably gold-digging in California).

> She lived her life; she did not dream it, think it, hope for it, or regret her inability to experience it. She had the gift of actualising her ambitions. Such a character as hers must always rouse one's admiration . . .[18]

I'm tempted at this point to steal away from the admirable to investigate another group of women who had a different talent for 'actualizing ambitions' – those sharp-shootin' gals of the old Wild

West. I don't mean the famous ones like restless adventurer Martha Jane Cannary (Calamity Jane), or Phoebe Mozee (Annie Oakley), renowned for her deadly marksmanship and sweet nature. I mean the real 'wildcats':[19] dedicated, career crooks.

The Wild West[20] was a place without precedent for enterprising women, harshly pragmatic and risky. It would be too simplistic to suggest that only outlaws could make a living there: despite its social history being littered with tantalizingly shadowy figures like 'Madame Moustache', a spectacularly successful gambler in 1850s Nevada, or 'Poker Alice' and 'Kitty the Schemer',[21] there was still room for legitimate enterprise, and plenty of women to take advantage of that. I shall come to them in due course: they do not belong here with the rebels. But the raw lawlessness of settlements on the rolling borders of civilized America drew the wayward of both sexes. Women who set up as brothel-keepers or saloon-owners were often highly skilled entrepreneurs; their businesses have already been documented and explored. But there were individual opportunists in these new-born towns and cities, too, like two of the ungentlest crooks of all: Belle Starr and Pearl Hart.

Belle (1848–89) was born Myra Shirley, the daughter of a Missouri judge, and should not have had to work for her living at all. Like Loreta Velasquez she found herself irresistibly aroused by the Civil War in 1861, and she used to go out scouting with her soldier brother, continuing to operate on the fringes of the Confederate forces after his death.

When the war ended Belle's family moved to Texas, where she eloped with the outlaw Jim Reed,[22] thus exchanging her respectable and no doubt restrictive birthright for rebellion. Unfortunately Reed was shot in the course of his travails as a highway robber, leaving Belle to work alone. She set herself up as the manager of some livery stables in Dallas, which fronted a dealership in stolen horses, and then married a Cherokee and settled down as Mrs Starr in a cosy little log cabin in Arkansas. Not long afterwards, however, their home became the headquarters of what was rumoured to be a network of outlaws run by Belle herself, and, like Reed, she too was shot dead, killed in action. She was forty-one.

Pearl Hart's career was a little more varied. She is supposed to have been born in Ontario (when, we do not know),[23] and run away from home soon after her marriage at sixteen, leaving both husband and baby behind. In 1893 she was enthralled by a Wild West Show she watched at the Chicago World Fair (where she was probably working as a peddler or pick-pocket), and when the performers left the city, she went too. It was then that she learned to smoke the opium to which she soon became addicted.

Pearl's lover from the show deserted her at some stage, and she turned to prostitution for a while. Then she drifted through Colorado and Arizona as a cook, a hotel maid, and professional gambler, eventually settling on highway robbery as the most gratifying way in which to earn a living. She would pose by the roadside in alluring distress and disarray; a stage-coach would gallantly stop to offer help, whereupon Pearl would draw a couple of revolvers from her bodice and together with her partner, John Boot, clean out the coach and its passengers. Boot was a bad choice, though, as it was his weakness and criminal ineptitude (according to Pearl) that landed them both in jail.

The trial was a show in itself. Pearl screamed at the judge her refusal to submit to so-called justice: 'I shall not consent to be tried under a law which my sex had no voice in the making!' She staged an overdose when sentenced (snorting on this occasion a sizeable pile of talcum-powder), and made life hell for the warders and prisoners by screaming obscenities day and night, although some of this uproar may well have been the involuntary result of cold turkey. On one occasion Pearl succeeded in scraping a hole in the prison wall just large enough to squeeze through and escape, but she was recaptured and not released again until she had served a five-year stretch.

As the sentence progressed – soon after the ineffectual Boot was released early due to good behaviour, in fact – Pearl decided to reform. Instead of screeching obscenities, she turned to prayer and started warbling hymns. She extolled the patent virtues of repentance and remorse, and vowed that when she had paid her dues, she would begin a new and useful life as a good woman. Yet within two years of her release in 1902, Pearl was arrested again on a charge of 'complicity with thieves'. This time there was too little evidence to convict her, and the authorities – probably with great relief – let her go.

Some say Pearl retired to Kansas City to run a cigar store; others have her joining a vaudeville show. No one tells us what happened to her in the end, though: she seems to have settled, uncharacteristically, for obscurity.

Before leaving America I should just mention one more character: a true heroine, this time, and one as proud of her country as it became of her. I suggested earlier that I did not want to write about America's lady-professionals. Being rather fond of the exceptions that prove rules, however, I am going to include a lady-doctor. Principally because she was not *just* a lady-doctor.

Unlike many of the ungentlewomen in this chapter, Mary Edwards Walker (1832–1919) never disguised herself as a man. She accepted her femininity, but refused to be bound by its conventions. She did not wear what women were supposed to wear, for example, believing jackets and trousers to be healthier, more comfortable and more practical than bodices and skirts. When she married, she did not take her husband's surname, preferring partnership to implied ownership. And when she decided what to do with her life, she went beyond the expectations of her age by choosing to be a surgeon.

Mary was not the first woman to qualify as a medical practitioner in America. Elizabeth Blackwell famously took that honour in 1849. In fact Mary's medical school at Syracuse, New York State, welcomed female as well as male students, as long as they had their parents' consent (rare for most women) and the necessary funds to pay for the course. Blessed with an enlightened father, Mary graduated in 1855, and a year later set up a practice in Rome, not far from Syracuse, with her husband Albert Miller. But the patients of rural New York were not ready for her. She wore trousers under her skirts, and it hardly sounded as though she and Dr Miller were married at all, otherwise why was she not Dr Miller too? The practice did not flourish – and neither did the marriage.

In 1861 Mary tried to enlist in the Union Army as a surgeon. She was qualified, but the need was not yet great enough to justify the freakish expedient of commissioning a woman, and so she volunteered instead, and was allowed to assist her male colleagues as a nurse. As the war advanced, however, she worked with increasing responsibility and closer and closer to the front lines (including Bull Run) until eventually, in 1862, she was appointed an assistant surgeon of the 52nd Ohio Infantry. Now the skirts disappeared altogether, rarely to return.

Mary relished her job, and excelled in a dangerous and eventful career with such panache that in 1865 she became the only woman to be awarded her beloved country's Congressional Medal of Honour: the highest available accolade. Even though the award was rescinded in 1917 (along with some 900 others), when it was decided it had been granted too profligately before, Mary wore her medal proudly, and daily, until the end of her life.

After the war she concentrated on writing and lecturing about her army career and her progressive medical and feminist theories. She visited England in 1866 to give an address on behalf of the National Dress Reform Association, clad in full male evening dress, including the top hat, and I suppose it is for this perceived eccentricity that she was best remembered until 1977, when her medal was officially restored to her posthumously by President Carter in recognition of her gallantry, dedication, and loyalty to her country.

Far more famous than Mary Walker on this side of the Atlantic is the first woman to have graduated from a British medical school: Dr Barry. But again, it is not for this distinction alone that she is so remarkable, but for the circumstances of her entire career which she spent, to all intents and (most) purposes, as a man – a meagre little smooth-skinned, mincing man, but a man, in a man's world, nonetheless.

It was in Dr Barry's interests, of course, to obfuscate the details of her early life, and she was as meticulously thorough in this as in all other aspects of her career. Her biographers have managed to tease out a few feasible assumptions from the confusion, though.[24] These suggest that Barry was a daughter of Mary Bulkley, sister of the Irish artist James Barry. Our Barry would have been born in about 1795, and taken in hand by her uncle when her mother Mary, encouraging her daughter's bizarre and dangerous determination to become a doctor, applied to him for help.

Like his sister, James Barry did not have much money, but he did have influential friends amongst his own patrons. One of them, David Erskine Steuart, Earl of Buchan, was a perfect ally for the girl: he admired the Bluestockings, and had a particular sympathy for Mary Wollstonecraft, once writing in her support that it was no wonder ladies were at a disadvantage in life for: 'The men of Europe have crushed the heads of women in their infancy, and then laugh at them because their brains are not so well ordered as they desire.'[25] No doubt delighted by the chance to work a little constructive subversion, he pulled whatever strings were necessary to enrol his protégée – a slight, long-nosed, rather lugubrious-looking Irish girl of fourteen – into the Medical School at Edinburgh University.

Another progressive patron of her uncle's, the exiled Venezuelan revolutionary and intellectual, Francisco de Miranda, undertook to provide the girl with a library, and when the time came to reinvent herself completely, she signed her full name as James Miranda Steuart Barry, in tribute to the three men who had helped her become what she was.

Although her gender may have been unusual, her young age was not so uncommon in the circumstances: medical training was not a post-graduate affair then, and there was no lower limit for university entry. James (as I shall have to call her from now on) lived with her mother, officially designated her aunt, while studying; she was privately tutored in Latin at home, to cover up the deficit occasioned by her not having been taught it at school, and in 1813 presented her thesis, in Latin, on hernias of the groin. It went down very well.

After a stint learning military surgery at the Edinburgh Royal Infirmary, James moved with her mother to London to become a 'pupil dresser', or surgeon's apprentice, at St Thomas's Hospital. In 1813 she enlisted in the Medical Department of the Army, and three years later received her first substantial appointment as Assistant Surgeon at the Cape. She was about eighteen.

James was not popular – on a personal level popularity was dangerous; professionally, it might mean making concessions, and she was never interested in that. During the twelve years she spent in South Africa she stirred things up amongst the colonial establishment to a most uncomfortable degree. She refused to take medical (or social) advice from her elders and supposed betters, often sweeping aside old medicines and methods to treat the sick in her own brusque and innovative way. Where others favoured over-elaboration, especially when dealing with an exalted patient, James practised simplicity and, wherever possible, promoted preventative medicine and common sense. She was a reformer, who treated lepers and prisoners and the mentally ill with as much sympathy, or more, as she treated the officers and officials of the Cape, and who made a point of speaking to the black and 'coloured' people she met, which outraged the politically sensitive. But she was a good doctor: she effected cures when hope had been lost, and for that she was admired.

The Governor of the Cape Colony, Lord Somerset, admired her particularly. She had more or less resurrected his daughter on one occasion, and the rumour was that James and Somerset became a good deal closer to each other than was proper. Fuelled, no doubt, by political machination, a full-scale scandal erupted when in 1825 Somerset sued for libel following accusations that he had committed 'an unspeakable atrocity with . . . the household physician', James Barry.

James eventually resigned. Not just because of the case, with its implicit charge of sodomy, but because she had already been sentenced to prison for conduct unbecoming to an officer and a gentleman, having failed to govern her white-hot temper (once lopping off someone's ear in a fit of pique) and consistently going over the heads of her superiors if she saw fit. Perhaps prudently, she seems to have taken a long furlough, and did not surface again until 1829, this time in Mauritius. Two years later she was posted to Jamaica (where she *must* have come across Mary Seacole's family: she even appointed a Creole matron in the hospital there . . .). She had learned no lessons of diplomacy from her past mistakes, however, and was court-martialled in Kingston for insubordination, which resulted in demotion and a posting to the Windward and Leeward Islands, otherwise known at the time as the abode of death.

James barely survived this next posting: when she thought she was dying of yellow fever, she issued instructions that her body should not be examined after her demise, but buried immediately, fully clothed. She recovered, however, and, after thirty years' service, and with her vitriolic spirit somewhat diluted by the Caribbean climate, Barry was promoted again in 1846 to Deputy Inspector-General of Hospitals and sent to Malta. Then came Corfu, and in 1855, at the height of the action, a holiday in the Crimea, where she came across Miss Nightingale, and saw fit to criticize her for some aspect or other of her hospital management:

> I never had such a blackguard rating [dressing down] in my life – I who have had more than any woman – than from Barry sitting on his horse while I was crossing the hospital square with only my cap on in the sun. He kept me standing in the midst of a crowd of soldiers, commissariats, servants, camp followers, etc., every one of whom behaved like a gentleman during the scolding I received while he behaved like a brute.[26]

There was something obviously ungallant about this five-foot figure, dressed in high-heeled boots with platformed soles, with the whining voice, the termagant temper, the lack of social and even professional nicety. Throughout her career, people commented on James's small white hands, her 'woman's touch', the way she walked, the shape of her hips, even her fondness for a small lap dog called Psyche she kept by her all the time. But the penny did not drop – with a very few, well-guarded exceptions[27] – until after her death in 1865. She succumbed to bronchitis in London after a final and cruelly cold appointment in Canada. The Staff Surgeon who attended her during her final illness was asked to write a report:

> I had been intimately acquainted with [Dr Barry] for a good many years both in the West Indies and in England . . . On one occasion after [his] death, I was sent for to the office of Sir Charles McGregor (Army Agents) and there the woman who performed the last offices for Dr Barry [i.e. who laid her out] was waiting to speak to me . . .
>
> Amongst other things she said Dr Barry was a female

and that I was a pretty doctor not to know this and that she would not like to be attended by me . . . She then said that she had examined the body and it was a perfect female and that there were marks of her having had a child when very young. I enquired: how have you formed that conclusion? The woman, pointing to the lower part of her stomach said 'From marks here . . . I am a married woman and the mother of nine children and I ought to know.'[28]

The official line thereafter was that 'James' had probably been a hermaphrodite, and her Army records were carefully lost. That she did ever have a child is unlikely, although some allude to the alleged affair with Somerset in the Cape, and her subsequent disappearance for a year or so . . . I guess she would hardly have welcomed working motherhood, and would have been well satisfied with the epitaph Florence Nightingale bestowed when she heard of the doctor's death:

I should say she was the most hardened creature I have ever met throughout the army.[29]

I have scoured Mary Seacole's book for some mention of Barry at the British Hotel in the Crimea: I should love to know what the warm-hearted, plain-speaking Jamaican had to say about the pursed-up doctor. Mary certainly did not hold back when describing my final 'ungentlewoman', whom she had the misfortune to meet on the isthmus of Panama in 1853:

Occasionally some distinguished passengers passed on the upward and downward tides of rascality and ruffianism, that swept periodically through Cruces. Came one day, Lola Montes, in the full zenith of her evil fame, bound for California, with a strange suite. A good-looking, bold woman, with fine, bad eyes, and a determined bearing; dressed ostentatiously in perfect male attire, with shirt-collar turned down over a velvet lapelled coat, richly-worked shirt-front, black hat, French unmentionables [trousers], and natty, polished boots with spurs. She carried in her hand a handsome riding-whip, which she could use as well in the streets of Cruces as in the towns of Europe; for an impertinent American, presuming – perhaps not unnaturally – upon her reputation, laid hold jestingly of the tails of her long coat, and as a lesson received a cut across his face that must have marked him for some days. I did not wait to see the row that followed, and was glad when the wretched woman rode off the following morning.[30]

Lola Montez was at this stage an infamous woman of thirty-two with a spectacular career as an adventuress behind her, and more extravagance still to come. There is a wonderfully louche photograph of her taken at about this time, showing a loose-jacketed, insolent-looking woman leaning on the back of a chair with a cigarette in her fingers. Lola was out to shock.

She reminds me of Becky Sharp in Thackeray's *Vanity Fair*: impulsive, manipulative and utterly self-centred. Elizabeth Rosanna Gilbert (she only became Lola later) had an itinerant upbringing. She was born in Ireland but lived for the most part in India – her father and stepfather being in the Army – and at school in Bath or with relations in Scotland. When she was sixteen she married Thomas James, an officer almost twice her age, and went with him to Karnal in India in 1839, quickly gaining a reputation amongst the ladies and gentlemen of the station – or two reputations: amongst the ladies as someone dangerously beautiful and morally dubious,[31] and amongst the gents as a game and spirited gel, always up for a bit of fun.

In 1840, Eliza was sent back to England for a while, ostensibly to convalesce after a fall while out riding, but one suspects that really she was desperate for some fresh air. Her marriage had become stale, and her talent to amuse was being stifled in the close-knit confines of station life. As soon as she broke free, she flourished, conducting a flagrant affair during the voyage home with nineteen-year-old George Lennox, nephew of the Duke of Richmond, and declaring her intention to live with the lad on their return to London.

James sued Lennox – and Eliza – for divorce, which was granted on the significant terms that neither of the Jameses should marry again, and for the first time in her life (Lennox by now having left her) Eliza was left to fend for herself.

But sharing the sort of spirit that sent Artemisia out to fight the Greeks, or Pope Joan off to university in Athens, Eliza refused to be average. She refused to dwindle into disreputable anonymity, and instead reinvented herself. Thanks to some of the connections she had made while Lennox's paramour, she took a course of Spanish lessons, engaged a dancing master, paid a preparatory visit to Cadiz, and emerged as Maria Dolores de Porris y Montez, indigent widow of a (real) recently executed hero of the Spanish resistance, Don Diego Leon. (How Lola got away with such a lie for so long is *very* hard to explain.) As Doña Maria Dolores, she took to the stage, and developed an act which soon became famous. 'Lola Montez, the Spanish Dancer' would make her career out of being adored.

Her smouldering performances in London, backed by various indulgent aristocrats, drew the great and the good. An advance notice of her appearance at Her Majesty's Theatre on 3 June 1843 was suitably fulsome:

> Donna Lolah Montes, who makes her debut to-night upon this stage, will for the first time introduce the Spanish dance to the English public . . . The French danseuse executes her pas with the feet, the legs, and the hips alone. The Spaniard

dances with the body, the lips, the eyes, the head, the neck, and with the heart. Her dance is the history of a passion . . . Lolah Montes is a purely Spanish dancer . . . The head lifted and thrown back, the flashing eye, the fierce and protruded foot . . . make a subject for the painter which would scarcely be easy to forget.[32]

But after a few more shows, during which it was noticed by the more level-headed of the critics that this was hardly a virtuosic display, rumours began to circulate that Donna Lola was none other than that saucy little Eliza James George Lennox had mixed himself up with. Lola flatly denied it, but was glad enough to leave London when invited to Germany by the bachelor Prince Heinrich of Leipzig for a command performance. She went on to tour Dresden, Berlin and Warsaw – to mixed reviews and with a diminishing band of true admirers (thanks to her petulance and ill temper) – before settling in 1846 in Munich under the besotted patronage of King Ludwig I of Bavaria.

She did not leave Ludwig for two years. Lacking an income from stage performances and obliging lovers, she was only too pleased to accept all he offered her, and while luxuriating as his consort, she developed a keen (though egocentric) interest in Bavarian politics. So resentful were Ludwig's peers of her influence, in fact, that revolution threatened, and eventually even he came to realize that Lola's ambitions were too costly to indulge. Lola returned to London in 1848, having failed to persuade the King to leave his country and family for her, and satisfied as a sort of consolation prize with a title (she was now the Countess of Landsfeld) and a generous allowance.

Pastures new: her next adventure involved marriage to a rich young gentleman called George Heald (having first ascertained that Ludwig's allowance would continue), swiftly followed by a warrant for her arrest on a charge of bigamy; then, even more swiftly, she left London for the Continent again to resume her dancing career, before diversifying into acting and touring the eastern states of America in a five-act play written for her and called, predictably enough, *Lola Montez in Bavaria*.

The critics were not kind: America was not fond of adventuresses passing themselves off as respectable victims of life's vicissitudes. So off she went again, sloughing off another old identity in favour of a new and more promising one – and that is when she met Mary Seacole. She was on her way to San Francisco, where she married for the third time. Strictly speaking, this marriage to Patrick Hull may not have been a bigamous one: her original, and legally her only, former husband Thomas James, had died at last, and while Heald was still alive, her union with him had never been legal anyway. Such punctilio would not concern Lola, though, and she blithely travelled with Hull to Grass Valley, California, to find a nice, restorative fortune in the goldfields.

She was unlucky, and despite settling in a demure white cottage Hull had found for her, and enjoying playing with the grizzly bear-cub and the pianola he somehow managed to produce for her amusement, the Countess of Landsfeld was bored. There wasn't any gold and there wasn't any excitement in Grass Valley, and so she left – for Australia. She was touring with her own company of players now, to the usual lukewarm reception, and taking casual lovers, until one of them, Frank Folland, drowned himself. People said it was suicide. On his death, the remorseful Lola underwent a sort of spiritual revolution, and spent the remaining five years of her life touring America and lecturing on such seemly subjects as 'Beautiful Women' and 'Heroines of History'. She raised money while doing so for Folland's widow and children, and for a church and an asylum for fallen women in New York, as well as for herself. She died of a stroke in Manhattan in 1861, exhausted at the age of thirty-nine.

Towards the end of her life, Lola was eloquent about the social and political frustrations of being an active and ambitious female.

The Company of Undertakers

Beareth Sable, an Urinal proper, between 12 Quack-Heads of the Second & 12 Cane Heads Or, Consul-tant. On a Chief Nebulæ, Ermine, One Compleat Docter issuant, cheekie Sustaining in his Right Hand a Baton of the Second. On his Dexter & sinister sides two Demi-Docters, issuant of the second; & two Cane Heads issuant of the third; The first having One Eye conchant, to-wards the Dexter Side of the Escocheon; the Second Faced per pale proper & Gules, Guardent. —— With this Motto ——————— Et Plurima Mortis Imago.

ET PLURIMA MORTIS IMAGO

Price Six pence

William Hogarth's design for a 'Quack-Head' coat-of-arms, featuring
osteopath 'Mad Sally', or Sarah Mapp (*top middle*)

WONDERFUL ADVENTURES
of
Mrs SEACOLE

LONDON
JAMES BLACKWOOD
PATERNOSTER ROW.

Mary Grant Seacole was a nurse, hotelier, restaurateur and irrepressible
entrepreneur in the Caribbean, Panama and the Crimea

Adventuress Lola Montez looking unwontedly demure on the cover of her autobiography (1858)

A woman miner is enriched by the jewels of wisdom and wealth her work
uncovers in this allegorical medieval miniature

THE PICTORIAL WORLD

AN·ILLUSTRATED·WEEKLY·NEWSPAPER

No. 7. Vol. I. {Registered at the General / Post Office as a Newspaper}   *SATURDAY, APRIL 18th, 1874.*   **THREEPENCE.** Per Post, 3½d.

WIGAN COLLIERIES: WOMEN WORKING AT THE COAL SHOOTS.

The reality of mining pictured here in Wigan in 1874, was altogether more brutish

(*Left*) Pearl Hart, who forged an intermittently successful career as a gambler and stage-coach robber in Colorado and Arizona

(*Below*) Victoria Woodhull with her sister Tennessee Claflin, the 'Lady Brokers' of Wall Street. Victoria ran for the Presidency of the United States in 1872

THE LADY BROKERS DRIVING THE BULLS AND BEARS OF WALL STREET.   TENNIE C. HOLDING THE REINS,
VICTORIA THE WHIP
(From ā cartoon in the *New York Telegraph*, February 18, 1870)

This page and page following: Three of Pandora's most enterprising daughters

(*Left*) Professional mountaineer Annie Smith Peck in her borrowed (and splendidly moustached) climbing mask

(*Below*) Zazel the Human Cannonball (fired nightly during the 1876 circus season in London)

Tattoo saleswoman Edith Burchett

'What can a woman do out there who cannot take her part?', she asked in her autobiography.

> Alas! for a woman whose circumstances, or whose natural propensities and powers, push her forward beyond the line of the ordinary routine of female life . . . Many a woman who has had strength to get outside of that line has not possessed the strength to stand there; and the fatal result has been that she has been swept down into the gulf of irredeemable sin. The great misfortune was that there was too much of her to be held within the prescribed and safe limits allotted to woman; but there was not enough to enable her to stand securely beyond the shelter of conventional rules.[33]

I wonder if it ever occurred to Lola to begin to change the rules, to move the boundaries of convention, rather than expend all her energy on breaking out of them? In retrospect, it seems obvious that when she died, in the latter third of the nineteenth century, the time *must* have been ripe for reform. Enfranchisement was beckoning: surely the woman eager to 'take her part' in the working world would be finding it easier to flourish and to be independent?

Unfortunately, the reality was very different. In the fifty-odd years it took for women to attain electoral equality it became, if anything, even more difficult than before to succeed as a self-respecting, self-sustaining woman.

7

OWNING ONESELF

I think a woman just as capable of making a living as a
man ... I don't care what society thinks; I have not time
to care ...

Tennessee Claflin[1]

WHY SHOULD IT HAVE BEEN SO DIFFICULT, as the nineteenth
century progressed, for respectable women to work unashamedly
for themselves? Was this not the most splendid, enlightened,
productive period yet in the history of the civilized world? All that
primitive misogyny of the Dark Ages was a distant memory. Girls
had a right to an education now as well as boys (thanks in part to
those impassioned petticoteries). Practical and charitable societies
were being run to foster a sense of self-worth and responsibility
in women. A rich provenance had developed of women earning
honourable livings – even pseudo-professional livings – to pave
the way for their daughters and granddaughters. It was an era
artistically in love with the past, reverently harking back to a Pre-
Raphaelite age when women were perceived to be both beautiful
and self-possessed. But at the same time it gazed with confidence
towards a shining future of commercial and industrial innovation

and success, redolent with the spirit of imperialism and protected by utter righteousness, in all of which women were *expected* to play their part. And, perhaps above all, there was once again a queen on the throne to remind England of its Elizabethan prowess, and the rest of the world of the gentle, invulnerable power of a lady with God on her side.

This was the great Victorian theory, but in practice things were different. First of all, the misogyny of the past was not completely dead and gone. It had just grown a little more subtle. One of the favourite periodicals of nineteenth-century Britain was a magazine called *Punch, or the London Charivari*, and it is littered with satirical cartoons, ridiculing women who aspired to independence. One issue I recall shows a china-doll-like lady slumped, exhausted, on a chair. Her husband leans solicitously over her, asking what can be wrong with his little 'Pippetywippety poppet'. It turns out she has spent all her strength on holding up a parasol to keep off the sun . . . The soft and milky rabble are back.

Even if ladies like Pippetywippety poppet possessed the stamina and moral fibre to succeed as useful working members of society, they were doomed:

> The brain and the frame of woman are formed with admirable suitability to their appropriate work, for which subtlety and sensitiveness, not strength and tenacity . . . are required. The cerebral organisation of the female is far more delicate than that of man; the continuity and severity of application needed to acquire real *mastery* in any profession, or over any science, are denied to women, and can never with impunity be attempted by them; mind and health would almost invariably break down under the task. And whenever any exceptional women are to be found who seem to be abnormally endowed in this respect, and whose power and mental muscle are almost

masculine, it may invariably, and we believe by a law
of physiological necessity, be observed that they have
purchased this questionable pre-eminence by a forfeiture
of some of the distinctive and most invaluable charms and
capabilities of their sex.[2]

Remember Aristotle and his theories on the weakness of
women?

Further down the social scale, the greatest sin a woman could
commit was still the wilful and pollutant sin of prostitution.
Poverty was a culpable social offence, and women who were
physically impoverished were too often assumed to be spiritually
bankrupt too.

Girls certainly did have a right to an education – or at least,
from 1891, to a free place at an elementary school between the
ages of five and twelve. Governesses abounded, of course, and if
a pupil's parents could pay, the private boarding- and day-schools
established from the seventeenth century onwards in almost every
town and city would cater to a genteel girl's every need, or rather
requirement. What was expected of an educated girl had not
changed much during the previous two or three hundred years,
and despite the efforts of such pioneers as Miss Buss of the North
London Collegiate School, and Miss Beale of Cheltenham Ladies'
College, both of whom were inspirational head teachers in the
1850s (and beyond), who taught their charges to esteem a good
brain as much as a kind heart, cosmetic accomplishment was
still prized above original thought. Needlework would regularly
be timetabled for the girls in elementary schools while the boys
did arithmetic, for example, and school inspectors were instructed
never to expect from girls what they would encourage from boys
in terms of mental agility and the ability to concentrate.[3]

It is true, vocational (as opposed to professional) colleges of
secondary education for women were beginning to appear. Bed-
ford College in London, opened in 1849, was the first ladies'

teacher-training college to be run in part by women, and the Nightingale School for Nursing was set up some ten years later: both institutions turned out students ready for two of the lowest-paid vocations of all. In America, readier to sell an academic education to women for education's sake alone, Elmira Female College became the first institution to award academic degrees, for what they were worth, in 1855, and the prestigious Vassar College was founded in 1865, with Maria Mitchell as its Professor of Astronomy, long before Oxford's Somerville or Newnham in Cambridge (both founded in 1879).

But what could be done with a university-educated woman any-way? In 1916 *Punch* offered a few suggestions in a cartoon called 'What Will She Become?', depicting a series of rather terrifying and deeply unattractive females: one staggered hopelessly up some steps with an enormous sack of flour over her shoulder; another wore ridiculous breeches and was felling trees; yet another sat furrow-browed over a volume of the *Scientific Wheatgrower*; and perhaps most usefully of all, a particularly ascetic-looking woman sat, with a look of earnest concentration, teaching a dog to beg.

Professional qualification was thus still a struggle. Medicine's bastions fell first, I suppose, but the law, the Church of England, architecture, accountancy, and so on, did not generally admit, never mind welcome, women for a very long time. The more regulated these professions became as far as entrance qualifica-tions were concerned, the less likely it was that women could take advantage of them. In fact, regulation in all walks of life, certainly in ultra-orthodox Victorian Britain, tolled the death knell for the sort of enterprising women who might have flourished in previous centuries. The odd female might be honoured with fellowship of some academic or scientific institution – as Caroline Herschel was, for example, or Mary Anning – but only as a special exception.

So much for education: both as a right for women and a vocation for them, it had grave and deep-rooted limitations.

What about all those Societies and Associations and Unions that characterize the nineteenth century? If a woman alone could do something, with prayers and her own conscience to guide her, to encourage industry and probity in others (particularly other women and children), think how much more effective a group of them would be. Modern, practical petticoteries, where not only were words spoken but deeds done, might be genuine agencies of change. In a society stratified by various degrees of spiritual and temporal superiority, moneyed men held the high ground, but moneyed women were not that far beneath them, and it was their business to make sure the milk of human kindness seeped even further down to reach 'the unfortunate' through charity.

Organization was the great thing, and the scope of these societies was bewildering. Many, I fear, were so limited in their remit, and so out of touch with what was really needed to advance the causes they espoused, that they soon evaporated altogether. Indeed, they had probably only been founded in the first place to keep idle women busy. Others, like the Society for the Promotion of the Employment of Women (1859) and, of course, the Women's Institute (1896), were effective, particularly those set up to target other women, either as benefactors or beneficiaries. The political unions spring to mind, campaigning for women's suffrage and culminating in enfranchisement in New Zealand in 1893, in Britain in 1918, and across America in 1920.[4] But other unions were working in less glamorous fields, some of the most constructive being employment agencies founded both at home and abroad.

In the end, it seemed to come down to the problem of what to do with what were ungallantly called in one publication, Britain's 'Old Maids'.[5]

If the surplus female population with which we are overrun increases much more, we shall be eaten up with women.

What used to be our better self will become our worst nine-tenths; a numerical majority which it will be vain to contend with and which will reduce our free and glorious constitution to that most degrading of all despotisms, a petticoat government ... The daughters of England are too numerous and if their mother cannot otherwise get them off her hands, she must send them abroad into the world.[6]

There *were* more women than men at home in Britain in the second half of the nineteenth century:[7] so many men were already working, fighting, or dying out in the Empire. Outfits like the Female Middle Class Emigration Society, the Self-Help Emigration Society or the United Englishwomen's Emigration Association aimed to do something productive about the imbalance, by populating the Empire with useful, independent workers.[8] Caroline Chisholm (1808–77) was a leading light in this movement to export women to the mutual benefit of themselves and their country. Having visited Australia in 1838 and been appalled at the physical and moral state of the women transported there as comparatively petty criminals, or as voluntary but ill-prepared emigrants, she made it her business to set up employment 'depots' up and down the coast of New South Wales, matching newly arrived workers with settlers' needs. Caroline's success encouraged other agencies, attracting ambitious and educated women as well as domestic staff to venture a self-sustaining life away from the stifling precedents of home. As we shall see later on, several of them flourished amazingly.

Some of these Societies did indeed help women find independence – but only, usually, if they were run by women themselves (the majority were not), and especially if they were able to place them in a new and comparatively unrestricted environment.

Did the undeniable strength of British commerce and industry affect prospects for respectable working women? The Industrial Revolution had not helped much. Even though the mills and the factories were full of mothers and daughters, their hours and conditions were appalling.

In America things were a little different. Its industrial revolution came a generation later, and quickly established a healthier environment, both physically and politically, for the factory girl, with the much-publicized Female Labor Reform Association[9] doing much towards limiting weavers' working hours to ten a day. Women industrialists seem to have been able to operate far more successfully in the fresh air across the Atlantic than in the black-bricked streets of the British north. Rebecca Lukens (1794–1854), for example, ran an iron-works in Pennsylvania which, under her direction, manufactured plates for locomotives and steam-ships, and which by 1957, under the management of her grandchildren, had become the largest iron-plate mill in the world. A glimpse at the catalogue of the Centennial Exhibition held in Philadelphia in 1876 shows in the 'Women's Pavilion' an impressive range of inventions, from Sarah Ball's and Mary Jackson's gas smoothing-iron to Caroline Brooks's 'Method of producing lubricated molds in plaster'. Other inventions included Margaret Plunkett's 'Triumph rotary washing machine', Mrs French's various 'electrotherapeutic appliances' and Charlotte Sterling's dishwasher – all of which were patented.[10]

Meanwhile, and much more prosaically, a visitor to Birmingham noted women nail-makers with surprise,[11] and female blacksmiths, braziers and the odd tin-plate worker occasionally surface in rural trade directories of the period.

There were women mine-workers too, not allowed underground (for reasons more of superstition than safety: a female down a mine shaft was considered about as lucky as a one on board ship).[12] Instead they sat from before dawn till after dusk sorting and grading the coal when it reached the surface, or else they picked at open seams. But depressingly, in Victorian England, instead of being admired for how hard they worked, or thanked for their application to a ghastly job (even if they had no choice but to do it), or even recommended as subjects ripe for reform, women were regarded as pernicious agents of immorality. A journalist for the *Pictorial World* explained why, headlining his piece 'Woman Miners in Male Attire':

> Picking my way through piles of ashes, muddy pools, and dilapidated coal trucks, I reached the edge of a vast mass of seemingly useless rubbish, from the summit of which I beheld a spectacle so utterly repugnant to my feelings, and according but ill with the character of the age. In various directions might be witnessed women with bare arms, one or two with short pipes in their mouths, performing labours totally unsuited to their sex. All were attired in male habilliments, but some had thrown aside their coats and jackets, and merely wore coarse shirts and trousers.[13]

Another commentator elaborated, claiming that because these women were dressed like this, they were manifestly guilty of enticing men to prostitutes. A man's dress on a woman, he said, 'drowns all sense of decency'; this allied to these girls' obvious lustiness of body and griminess of soul could only lead to 'the grossest immorality'.[14]

I'm not so naive as to suggest that these pit girls might not have grabbed at any opportunity to get themselves off the coal face and into some gentler means of earning a living. But nor do I think they can have lacked some pride in what they did. Some of them used to arrange beads, feathers and fresh berries every morning around their bonnets, to leaven the dirt and ugliness of their uniform.[15] It is patronising to assume that they chose to work as they did, to wear breeches, to roll up their sleeves and get their muscular arms dirty, just in order to corrupt Victorian gentlemen. Britain was still a long way off crediting its working women with any sense and sensibility.

I mentioned the spirit of imperialism that bathed Britain and so many other places around the globe in a comfortable glow. While it did provide practical opportunities for a number of adventurous women throughout the nineteenth century, it did not generally encourage independence. Take British India, for example: there the 'memsahib' – literally, the lady-master – was sent expressly to help transplant Britain abroad. She was supposed to embody all that was most prized by the expansionist British government: home values, duty, Christian comfort, and moral and sexual purity. Most of the British women abroad during the great age of Empire were, therefore, no more than political tools, as much subjects of imperialist rule as the natives amongst whom they lived. As Caroline Chisholm herself put it, they were there as 'God's Police',[16] or passive keepers of the public conscience.

As for Queen Victoria, she had better speak for herself. When faced with the possibility of a Bill for Women's Suffrage being passed by her Parliament in 1870, she responded unequivocally:

> The Queen is most anxious to enlist everyone who can speak or write to join in checking this mad, wicked folly of 'Woman's Rights', with all its attendant horrors, on which her poor feeble sex is bent, forgetting every sense of womanly feeling and propriety . . . [Women] should be sensibly educated – and employed wherever they can be usefully, but on no account unsexed and made doctors (except in one branch), lawyers, voters, etc. Do that, and you take away at once all their claim to protection on the part of the male sex.[17]

In this era, I had some difficulty in tracking down independent career women working untroubled behind the scenes of such a highly structured society. There are plenty of pioneers, striking out for political credibility or professional repute, but precious few working for themselves in occupations not traditionally deemed the province of women. To find them I had to look beyond the increasingly parochial shores of Britain, at emigrants, travellers – and Americans.

The emigrants and travellers first. Here is an extract from a letter written from Sydney Cove, Australia, in 1792:

> octb 8th 1792.
>
> my Dear aunt
>
> we arrived he[re] on the 7th and I hope it will answer better than we expected for I write this on Board of ship but it looks a pleasant Place-enough. [W]e shall but have 4 pair of trouser to make a week and we shall have a pound of rice a week and 4 pound of pork besides Greens and other vegetaibles . . . I will make myself as happy as I can [i]n my present and unhappy situation . . .
>
> . . . from your undutifull neice [sic] Mary Haydock.[18]

Mary was fifteen when she wrote this. Two years earlier she had been caught trying to sell a stolen horse near Stafford in England, and since there was no one to bail her out, or take her in hand (she had been orphaned as a baby and lived by her wits), her sentence was transportation aboard the *Royal Admiral* to Australia for seven years. 'I will watch every oppertunity to get away in too [sic] or 3 years,' she assured her aunt at home in Lancashire, but meanwhile, she had to shift for herself as best she could.

She managed to avoid spending too long sewing trousers by finding a place as a nursemaid soon after her arrival; in 1794, aged seventeen, she married Tom Reibey, a former employee of the Honourable East India Company, whom she had met on the *Royal Admiral*, and who had decided to settle in New South Wales as a general trader. He found in Mary an eager partner: her flair for business was gratifyingly evident in the ever-fatter returns the Reibeys won from an astonishing range of ventures. *And* she raised a family of seven children. Before Tom's death in 1811 the couple traded in grain, coal and timber, gradually expanding the size and number of vessels they owned until a whole fleet of ships was at their disposal. They farmed, they were seal-hunters, property-dealers, money-lenders, shop-keepers and hoteliers, and almost everything they did, they did in partnership.

After her husband's demise, Mary gathered the businesses to herself, expanding and developing them until much of Macquarie Place in Sydney, together with parts of George and Castlereagh Streets, were hers, as well as a number of farms on the Hawkesbury River and in Tasmania. She was like a modern-day Alice Chester: her money helped found Australia's first bank (the Bank of New South Wales), and her charity endowed schools and churches in the new-born city she had made her own.

It took a little longer than the 'too or 3 years' for Mary to come home again: she took two of her daughters back to Lancashire in 1820. But she did not stay: she died back in Sydney, where she had been happily living off her carefully and personally husbanded investments during her 'retirement', at the age of seventy-eight.

Well-respected as she is, the soubriquet of Australia's 'First Lady' is not usually applied to Mary these days: historians prefer Elizabeth Macarthur (?1767–1850) for that role.[19] Elizabeth arrived in Sydney Cove in 1790 – apparently the first free white woman to set foot in Australia[20] – and became first a sheep-farmer and then an exporter of fleeces (particularly from the merino flocks she established with her husband), dying, like Mary, a rich and commendably old woman. But I warm less to Macarthur than to Mary. The former was affluent and well educated; she volunteered to go to Sydney with her officer husband, and although she was undoubtedly a spectacularly successful businesswoman, and stoutly enjoyed her own efforts, I do not think she engaged in that raw fight for colonial survival that Mary did. Elizabeth was admirable, and so was Mary. But Mary was feisty too.

South Africa proved to be another good stamping-ground for the more spirited daughters of the Empire, although it does not feature until the mid to late nineteenth century (the Transvaal was annexed in 1877). It seems to have attracted women who, like Lola Montez, were a little too 'large' to be contained at home. Sarah Heckford (1839–1903) was one of them. Her autobiography[21] is full of ripping yarns and derring-do, detailing her unlikely life as a *smous*, or trader, on the veldt, interspersed with episodes of farming, speculation and spying. In fact, it is hard to believe it was written by the same person who had already spent a good lifetime, measured in Victorian terms, in London, struggling with ill-health and deformity (she had suffered a tubercular infection whilst a child, which left her hunch-backed and bronchitic). In those days she was married to a doctor and determined to qualify too; she nursed victims of cholera in the East End, and eventually established the East London Hospital: the first to admit babies and, bizarrely, dogs.[22] She was widowed in 1871. Her husband had contracted tuberculosis, and assured her with his dying breath that he would wait in the spirit world for her to follow him, as she would surely do, and soon, for she had TB too.

These were her circumstances, then, when she set off for South Africa at the age of thirty-nine. She had finally relinquished her ambition to become a doctor herself; she was tiny, weak and exhausted after a trip to India to do a little missionary work in memory of her husband, and no doubt prepared to meet the grim reaper. So she determined on an adventure before she went to her death, courageously hoping to wear herself out in the end, rather than slip gradually from the world.

Sarah travelled armed with 100 shares in the Transvaal Farming,

Mining and Trading Association: she wanted to study agriculture and land management there. For a while she lived as a governess with a farming family, but the land and climate seemed to have a beneficial effect and, suddenly feeling rejuvenated, she declared herself ready to 'leap the barriers of young-lady-dom', and look for a farm herself.

First she needed some capital: she invested in a wagon and span of bullocks, engaged three men to help her work them, stocked up with such necessities as pots and pans, haberdashery, crockery and so on, and set out onto the veldt to trade these goods with outlying settlers for ostrich feathers, hides, ivory, corn and dried meat. Any profit she made would be ploughed into her farming fund.

Sarah's timing was bad: just as she embarked on her temporary career as a *smous*, the Boer War began to simmer and British colonists started moving back to the local settlement of Pretoria for protection. She could still be useful, by carrying intelligence with her on her travels and reporting Boer movements to the authorities, but she could hardly make a living, let alone save anything. So, immediately after the siege of Pretoria in 1880, she sold up what little she still possessed and returned to London.

On the voyage home Sarah completed the manuscript for her autobiography. Then, still restless, she took herself back to the East End to put into practice some of her long-held socialist beliefs[23] by starting a workers' cooperative in Woolwich. She worked there herself until news of a massive gold strike near what was soon to become Johannesburg ineluctably drew her back to South Africa in 1886. For the next fifteen or so years, she lived there again, on and off, as – successively or concurrently – a mining-share broker, a trader, a farmer, a school-foundress, a writer of papers on sociology and education, and an accomplished lecturer.

She was sixty-two when her feeble little body gave up, but her questing spirit stayed lusty to the last. Had she stayed at home in London, I doubt whether she would have survived past forty.

[157]

Equally indomitable were three of nineteenth-century America's most astute businesswomen: Lydia Pinkham, Sarah Breedlove Walker and Victoria Woodhull. I cannot resist including them, not only by virtue of their originality and éclat as working women, but as examples – the first, I think – of true career women. I have used the term before rather loosely to mean women who support themselves (and often others) as independent workers; what a career really means, though, is 'a profession affording opportunities of advancement',[24] a skilled occupation in which one can progress, through flair and application, to ever greater success. And while an elaborate glass ceiling was sanctimoniously being constructed over the ambitions of real career women in England during the latter half of the century, the Americans Lydia, Sarah, and Mrs Woodhull, in the true spirit of Pandora's daughters, got on with it.

As a child, a favourite pop song was always 'Lily the Pink', by a group called the Scaffold. The words of the chorus went like this:

> We'll drink a drink, a drink,
> To Lily the Pink, the Pink, the Pink,
> The saviour of the human race;
> For she invented
> Medicinal Compound,
> Most efficacious in every case.

Only recently did I discover to my amazement that 'Medicinal Compound' really existed, and that 'Lily the Pink' was none other than Lydia Estes Pinkham (1819–83), whose elixir earned her some $300,000 per annum by the time of her death.

Lydia's career as a herbalist and businesswoman was a short but spectacular one. She trained originally as a school-teacher, then gave up salaried work when she married. Her husband dabbled ineffectually in real estate, but after the financial crash of 1873 –

by which time the Pinkhams had six children – they became near-destitute. Desperate to help, Lydia proposed trying to sell a herbal remedy she used to brew for friends and neighbours who complained of 'woman's weakness'. Her two sons covered the local area of Lynn, Massachusetts, with handbills and posters proclaiming the remedy's wondrous benefits, while their mother stirred cauldrons of nostrum like some modern-day Joanna Stephens, and by 1876, the fame of 'Mrs Lydia E. Pinkham's Vegetable Compound' had reached Boston, New York and beyond. Then, as now (more or less), the ingredients comprised various roots, including licorice and pleurisy (or butterfly-weed); dandelion, gentian, fenugreek seeds, and quite a bit of alcohol (18 per cent proof).

Lydia's acuity in sales and marketing was just as impressive as her medical intuition – if not more so. She patented a label for the $1 bottles of her compound, bought up space in newspapers, and wrote advertising copy herself, often illustrating it with her own portrait. There is a splendid trade card, adorned on one side with an engraving of the spanking new Brooklyn Bridge, from which is hanging a banner running the whole of its length advertising the Compound. On the verso is a description of Lydia Pinkham's 'Positive Cure', which recalls the quacks of old:

> It will cure entirely the worst form of Female Complaints, all Ovarian troubles, Inflammation and Ulceration . . . and is particularly adapted to the Change of Life.
>
> It will dissolve and expel tumours from the uterus in an early stage of development. The tendency to cancerous tumours there is checked very speedily by its use.
>
> It removes faintness, flatulency . . . cures Bloating, Headaches, Nevous Prostration, General Debility, Sleeplessness, Depression and Indigestion . . .
>
> For the cure of Kidney Complaints of either sex this Compound is unsurpassed . . . Six bottles for $5. Sent by

mail in the form of pills . . . Mrs Pinkham freely answers
all letters of inquiry. Send for pamphlet.[25]

These 'letters of inquiry' were dealt with by a 'Department of
Advice' (or an agony-aunt service) within the rapidly expanding
company, staffed entirely by females, for, as Lydia said, 'only a
woman can understand a woman's ills.'[26]

Like Mother Shipton, Lydia has her own website now. The company she founded was taken over, but it still sells the Compound
(as an alternative to hormone replacement therapy), based on the
original recipe, worldwide.

The accolade of being America's first self-made woman million-
aire goes not to Mrs Pinkham, as one might have expected, but to
the African-American Sarah Breedlove Walker (1867–1919). She
employed thousands of people across America in the early 1900s,
but began life as the orphaned daughter of a poor Louisiana farmer.
She was married at fourteen, and at twenty found herself a widow
with her own daughter, A'Leila, to support. She spent the next
eighteen years working as a washerwoman to send A'Leila through
college (unusual in itself) and dreaming of better things. It was a
dream, she always said, that inspired the business she started in
1905, soon after her second marriage to newspaperman Charles
Walker. A recipe for dressing black women's hair floated into her
mind one night, and when she put it into practice next morning,
it worked.

'The Walker Method' for shampooing, conditioning and
straightening hair had instant appeal. Although Sarah only began
demonstrating it door to door in 1906, by 1910 she had amalga-
mated two offices in Denver and Pittsburgh, and built a plant in
Indianapolis, 'on my own ground', churning out her preparations
and training the women she appointed as 'Hair Culturists' or agents
to spread the word across the continent. She organized 'Walker
Clubs' for these agents, promising prizes to the individuals and
clubs who raised the most money, not for the company but for

charity. She became a generous philanthropist for the benefit of African-American women, offering them alternative ways of earning an honourable and stimulating living, and endowing schools and colleges to educate them and so lead them, she devoutly hoped, into a new, enlightened age of equal rights for men and women, black and white.

This quest for equality was what motivated one of the highest-profile American women of all in her bid to take over the world – or the financial world, at least. Victoria Woodhull, *née* Claflin (1838–1927), reminds me of Lola Montez: she lived a perilously adventurous life, morally as well as physically and politically, and by force of personality alone she 'scaled the walls of fame' (as that eulogist of the Duchess of Newcastle put it) to sit squarely and defiantly on the top.

Victoria's life had never been ordinary. Born in Ohio of a fey and fervently religious mother, and a father who vacillated between gambling and farming, horse-trading and bar-keeping (none with much success), she grew up an intelligent, romantic and passionate girl. Her formal education was an intermittent and unsatisfying affair; it came to an end entirely when a local doctor proposed marriage and was accepted by Victoria's father on her behalf. Victoria was fourteen, and considered her life to be over.

It might well have been: Dr Woodhull was an alcoholic, usually out of work, and unfaithful. Their first child was mentally handicapped, condemned to imbecility, reasoned Victoria, by his loveless conception and squalid birth. Their second was delivered by Woodhull, but he was so incapable at the time that he forgot to tie the umbilical cord. The baby survived, however, to become Victoria's much-loved companion Zula. Victoria left Woodhull as soon as she was physically able, and went back to her family, soon joining her sister Tennessee (Tennie) on the road as a fortune-teller. Their father's latest enterprise was quackery: he advertised himself as Dr R. B. Claflin, 'American King of Cancers', and his daughters as spiritual healers and mediums.

[161]

We have not really touched on women mediums (as opposed to witches) since Mother Shipton but they were numerous and remarkably successful, especially during the nineteenth century. The pronouncements of spiritualism and theosophy seemed to favour the mouths of mysterious women, and if those women were, like Victoria, intense but somewhat stymied, acting as a medium offered a certain credibility, and an opportunity to influence and achieve. Victoria seems genuinely to have believed in her powers, supported as they were by visionary Christianity, and her passionate nature and strangely innocent-looking sultriness bought her attention, admiration and a living.

Victoria's second marriage in 1866 was to an upstanding gentleman by the name of Colonel Blood, so besotted that he gave up wife, family, kudos (he had been a war hero) and political ambition to be with her. Victoria divorced Woodhull to wed Blood, but it has been suggested that Blood neglected to reciprocate.[27]

Two years later, the defining moment of Victoria's career occurred. She met the fabulously opulent shipping magnate, Cornelius Vanderbilt, who rapidly became her patron and most ardent admirer. She and Tennie, who enchanted Vanderbilt even more, used to arrange private seances for him, and even went so far as to advise – on information, no doubt, from the other side – on his investments. They were paid for their services, of course, and with her new-found wealth and implied social prominence, Victoria determined to enter the business world herself.

She had a strong sense of theatre,[28] and a strong sense of self, too: I believe she was quite well aware of the impact a glamorous and intelligent woman was likely to make on Wall Street. Here she chose to make her debut in the financial market, after risking her savings from clairvoyancy fees on speculation in gold and surfacing with some $700,000 – or so she said – to invest elsewhere.

Her business acumen and flair for publicity were almost as effective as Lydia Pinkham's. Vanderbilt backed her and Tennie, who had come into the venture too, with money and his personal endorsement; interviews and advertisements were arranged in the newspapers; the sisters were careful to be seen as utterly feminine and apparently well-bred, with immaculate costumes and the odd fresh flower in the hair or on the bosom, while at the same time cultivating an image of blistering perspicacity and even gravitas. They were both 'self-owned' ladies, they claimed, and proud of it.

At first it did not hinder Victoria, although it was a risk, that she broadcast a passionate interest in women's suffrage, and attended the first convention of the National Woman Suffrage Association, addressed by pioneer feminist Elizabeth Cady Stanton, in 1869. She was flourishing proof that women could be taken seriously in a man's world while retaining their essential womanliness, and that Queen Victoria was wrong in insisting that powerful women must forfeit their femininity to succeed. She started a succession of newspapers to support both her business and political ambitions: *Woodhull and Claflin's Weekly* had the inevitable motto 'Onward and Upward', and espoused women's issues with as much vigour as it muck-raked around in business rivals' affairs.

But from the early 1870s, Victoria's good fortune began to curdle and turn sour. She took lovers injudiciously; she over-reached herself in her staggering ambition to become President of the United States (although she was nominated to run for the Equal Rights Party in 1872, and had already chosen the outfit she would wear when elected to victory); she overdid the emphasis she put on spiritualism in her personal and professional life, claiming a vocation to evangelize the healthiness of 'free love' and sexual emancipation.

Once her credibility in high American society began to crack, there was no stopping the rapid disintegration of her reputation. Court cases were brought against her for non-payment of debts, and for disseminating 'obscene literature' (i.e. a newspaper article detailing the sexual mores of some of her competitors on Wall Street). Her own advanced, though sincerely held, views on

[163]

'serial monogamy' outside marriage were gleefully publicized by detractors. Investors avoided her offices on Wall Street and her speculations bombed. Vanderbilt sensibly disentangled himself from her, and finally, broken in health if not quite in spirit, she left for London in 1877 to try another sort of life instead.

In England Victoria, still with her sister Tennie, called herself Mrs Woodhall. She did lecture tours, speaking about sexual education rather than liberation, and launched *Woodhall and Claflin's Journal* ('Devoted to the Advocacy of Great Social Questions and . . . the Improvement of Women') and *The Humanitarian* (a periodical disquietingly in favour of selective breeding and 'the aristocracy of the blood'). Tennie met a rich and adoring old industrialist called Francis Cook and married him; Victoria met an equally rich and adoring young banker called John Martin, and married *him*, and after a few twitches of the old political fervour – on one occasion going back to New York to stand again as a candidate for the presidency – she retired to rural Worcestershire in luxury and, one assumes, in peace.

8

OUT OF BOUNDS

A woman can hardly ever choose ... she is dependent on
what happens to her. She must take meaner things, because
only meaner things are within her reach.

George Eliot[1]

I'M NOT SURE WHY VICTORIA WOODHULL elected ultimately to
lead such a quiet life. It seems strange that such a combative
campaigner should settle for comfort and conformity quite as
solidly as she did. She never even used the vote she professed
to be so desperate to win for her sex: she would not be allowed
to in Britain, as an American citizen, and she was not in America
during the post-1920 elections for which she would have been
eligible. Perhaps she no longer needed a career or a crusade: she
had got where, and what, she wanted.

This is not a particularly common pattern amongst the women in
this book. It is hard to imagine Hypatia ever losing the enthusiasm
and intellectual generosity that hallmarked her university career
in fourth-century Alexandria, or Pope Joan deciding one day that
enough was enough, she'd had a good innings as pontiff, and it was
time to retire. I'm willing to bet that the entrepreneurial gardener

Juliana of Ely kept working as long as her weatherbeaten body allowed, and I know Christine de Pizan was still writing in 1429, a year before her death, her last recorded work being (characteristically) a song in honour of Joan of Arc. Moll Cutpurse was outrageous to the last second and beyond; Mary Wollstonecraft was a working mother who would have continued after the birth of her second daughter had she lived; Mary Anning only stopped her fossilizing when advancing breast cancer made it impossible to continue – and so on. They had heretical blood in their veins, these women, and they were free spirits all.

So Mary Ann Evans, masquerading as George Eliot, was wrong to say that a woman could never choose, and that femininity inevitably meant passivity, just like Jane Austen's Catherine Morland when she complained that there were 'hardly any women at all' in history. Here are plenty who have made choices, who have sought out independence, and who have reached well beyond the supposed limitations of their lives. The history of working women should not be confined, as it has tended to be for the past century or two, to the orthodox formula of *females + education = opportunity + precedent = collective liberty* (with a great void before the 'females + education' bit). Virginia Woolf in her feminist essay *A Room of One's Own* was guilty of this sort of over-simplification, insisting that 'intellectual freedom depends upon material things . . . And women have always been poor, not for two hundred years merely, but from the beginning of time.'[2] What about *females + sense of adventure = opportunity + bloody-mindedness = personal liberty*? This would be less overtly feminist, but much fairer to the people I have been discussing, who have all, to a greater or lesser degree, been living their lives out of bounds, and free (or ignorant) of social, cultural or political constraint.

In fact, some of them have been so unconstrained as to flummox my attempts to slot them into the body of this book. Where does a sixteenth-century Japanese spymaster fit in, for example?

Or a seventeenth-century purveyor of arsenic to murderous wives? The actress, sausage-seller and 'well-known trouble-maker' Charlotte Charke (died 1760),[3] or game-hunter and champion animal-stuffer Martha Maxwell (1831–81)? If only to prove how astonishingly diverse a range of careers have been available to women in the past, I am determined to include some of these most maverick of mavericks now, in this final chapter.

The first in line, chronologically, is Doña Marina, active in Mexico around 1520. She was the daughter of an Aztec chief; when her widowed mother married again and had a son, whom she preferred over her daughter, Marina was dispatched to a neighbouring tribe, the Xicalango. Marina's lofty heritage made her a desirable asset, and the Xicalango sold her to the Cacique, or military chief, of Tabasco, who in turn presented her with nineteen other women to the Spanish conquistador Hernando Cortés during his Mexican expedition of 'discovery' in 1517.

Marina's mother-tongue was the Aztec language of Nahuatl. But during her itinerant youth she had become fluent in the Mayan dialects of the Yucatan peninsula, and was able to translate for Cortés (through a Spanish-speaking intermediary) on his relentless progress through Mexico. He came to rely on her not just as his translator, but as a diplomat, advisor, mistress and eventually the mother of his son. Modern Mexicans either revile 'La Malinche', or 'the captain's lady', as a traitor for her part in helping to negotiate the conquest of the native Indians, or celebrate her insistence on Cortés's talking with the Indians rather than weighing in to slaughter them wholesale. The original chronicler of the 1517–21 expedition, eye-witness Bernal Diaz del Castillo, was reverential, writing that her help was instrumental in the growth of the Spanish Empire:

> This was the beginning of our conquests, and thus, praise be to God, all things prospered with us. I have made a

[167]

point of telling [her] story, because without Doña Marina
we could not have understood the language of New Spain
and Mexico.[4]

Cortés himself agreed: 'After God,' he said, 'we owe this conquest of New Spain to Doña Marina.'[5]

At the same time as the Doña was working her diplomacy, the
only recorded *conquistadora* was fighting on the front line. Maria
de Estrada embarked on this expedition from her home in southern
Spain with her husband, both having proved their mettle as soldiers
and surrendered the necessary (hefty) fee to join Cortés. Maria,
especially, distinguished herself at the battle of Tenochtitlán in
1519. She was apparently a swordswoman of devastating skill,
and was later invested with almost mythic qualities by the Indians
as well as by the Spanish.

That Japanese spymaster I mentioned, Chiyome (*fl.* 1560), set
up a training school in her home for ninja *kunoichi* girls, or 'deadly
flowers'. There she instructed them in the age-old techniques
of swift and efficient bloodshed, and embellished her espionage
classes with a staggering array of gadgets. Her pupils learned to
dip hairpins in poison, to hide grappling irons in their kimono
sashes, or to survive underwater for minutes at a time, before
graduating as some of Japan's deadliest spies and contract killers.
Chiyome then acted as their agent, hiring them out to samurai
warlords and the like. If they perished in the line of duty, no
matter: Chiyome recruited her *kunoichi* from the street, taking
in homeless or unwanted girls, thus breaking the ninja monopoly
that had been confined to certain families in particular Japanese
regions for generations. There were always plenty more pupils to
keep up the numbers, and I'm sure Chiyome grew fat on their
efforts.[6]

Another professional assassin was the Sicilian apothecary Tofana
(died *c.*1720). Her methods were, like Chiyome's, indirect: she
brewed poison for the use and benefit of frustrated wives. She

called her infusion 'Manna of St Nicholas of Bari', and labelled it (for those who did not need to know) as a miraculous remedy. In reality, 'Aqua Tofana' was a potent killer, responsible, they claimed at her trial in 1709, for some 600 deaths in and around Palermo.

This is turning into something of a rogues' gallery, and so is just the place for Charlotte Charke (1713–60), wayward daughter of the playwright Colley Cibber. Charlotte was a proud and anarchic tomboy in her youth, who, like Moll Cutpurse, is said to have delighted in 'strange mad pranks'.[7] Although put to work at fourteen to learn 'housewifely perfections', she nursed ambitions to become a quack, travelling the country selling balmy – or deadly – herbal potions, or perhaps a groom or gardener. Instead she married a theatre musician, and even though estranged from her father, she turned to the stage herself, thereafter leading a picaresque life as an actress (once playing the part of Pope Joan), a theatre-manager, writer, puppeteer and conjuror's assistant. She never lost her restlessness: as in the case of so many of these mavericks, she was driven to increasingly outlandish pursuits. She tried being a grocer and 'oil woman' in Covent Garden, then she opened a 'Stake and Soup-house' in Drury Lane, before becoming a pastry-cook. She enjoyed a brief career as a highwaywoman, under-taken primarily to give herself the chance to hold up and rob her own detested father, which she managed to do one night in Epping Forest. She had not been too proud to ask him for money in the past, but it was never forthcoming. The reply to one of her begging letters – probably the last – suggests why:

> Madam,
>   The strange career which you have run for some years (a career not always unmarked by evil) debars my affording you that succour which otherwise would naturally have

been extended to you as my daughter. I must refuse therefore . . .

Yours in sorrow,
Colley Cibber.[8]

Charlotte was a great believer in diversification. At various times during her hand-to-mouth existence she worked as a valet or 'superior domestic' (dressed as a man and calling herself, somewhat unimaginatively, Mr Brown), an imprisoned debtor, a farmer on the Welsh borders, a typesetter on a Bristol newspaper, and an itinerant sausage-seller on the streets of her native city of London. She kept herself alive for forty-seven years – not bad for the time – but never excelled. I think she would have liked to have excelled.

Another showgirl was the acrobat Zazel, one of an elusive number of Victorian circus ladies, who dazzled and deafened her audience during the 1876–7 season in Westminster by being repeatedly fired from the mouth of a cannon. In reality Zazel was an eighteen-year-old young lady called Miss Dunn, who worked in order to support her brother and herself. One cannot help wondering quite how and why she became a human cannonball.[9] But someone's got to do it, I suppose.

On the other side of the Atlantic, Idawalley Zoradia Lewis (1842–1911), better known as Ida, was celebrated throughout America for her strength and courage as a lifeboat-woman. And Annie Peck (1850–1935) was renowned for her prowess as a mountaineer. She conquered Popocatepetl (17,887ft) and Orizaba (18,700ft) in Mexico before making the first ascent of the north face of Peruvian Mt Huascaran (21,834ft) in 1908, and was desperate to be accepted as a professional, undertaking trigonometric and barometric experiments as she climbed and offering the results, in her books and papers, to various institutions for the edification of scientists and public alike. No one would commission her, needless to say, and she was even reduced on one occasion to fashioning a makeshift high-altitude mountaineering suit from an elderly eskimo kagoul loaned by the American Museum of Natural History, topped with a knitted mask on which was jauntily embroidered a fine moustache. Peck was ultimately a frustrated career mountaineer, but she certainly tried.

The 'Indian Agent' at Morongo in southern California in 1908 was a woman. Clara True was appointed to oversee the reservation there and administer its jail and school, as well as taking responsibility for the moral and physical welfare of the Native Americans within its boundaries. She was more than equal to the job, as her manifesto shows:

> It is my duty to make everybody happy if I can. There are too many people abroad who are not dispensing pleasure. I will get all the fun I can out of this myself, and try to divide up on smiles . . . I am going to keep well. I'm at a disadvantage in being an old maid, but if I get a case of nerves, I'll be unendurable. I'm going to be under control as to temper if possible, and if this is impossible, I'll bark at somebody who needs it.
>
> I recognize my dependence upon God for the blessings I need, but I do not expect him to furnish them ready-to-wear [for the Indians] nor pre-digested . . . Undigested creed is to the mind what green apples are to the stomach . . .
>
> If Heaven will send me a good friend and a good enemy, I'll get along.[10]

Back in Britain again, Emily Faithfull (1835–95) was a member of London's literati, and was particularly friendly with the feminist Bessie Rayner Parkes, founder and editor of the highly political *Englishwoman's Journal* in 1858. In 1859 Emily became Secretary of the newly formed Society for Promoting the Employment of Women (of which Parkes was also a committee member), and in 1860 she established the Victoria Press, expressly to put into practice her most passionately held belief that women of whatever social caste should be free to find skilled employment if they wished, or needed.

The Press took on men for the heavy work, shifting iron type frames and the like, but – in the style of some fifteenth-century Italian nuns of whom Emily had read – all the compositors were women. She appointed five apprentices on opening, and six months later was able to take another sixteen. In 1862 Queen Victoria granted Emily official approval by naming her 'Printer and Publisher in Ordinary to Her Majesty'. But the fledgling trade unions were less delighted by Miss Faithfull: her lady compositors were undercutting other printing houses and threatening to put *real* workers, i.e. men, out of business. Action had to be taken.

> The opposition was not only directed at the capitalist [Emily] but the girl apprentices were subjected to all kinds of annoyance. Tricks of a most unwomanly nature were resolved to, their frames and stools were covered in ink . . . the letters were mixed up in their boxes, and the cases were emptied of 'sorts' [characters] . . . Again and again the machinery was wilfully injured and destroyed, and the waste of capital was simply ruinous.[11]

One of the Press's employees did triumph in being admitted to the London Society of Compositors in 1892 (an association which saw fit to exclude women again in 1941), but the quality of Emily's training – and, indeed, her printing – was not generally considered first-rate. That, and the losses sustained by industrial sabotage, stopped the Victoria Press from flourishing as Emily would have wished, but she was justly proud of having established it, and of her best-known publication, the monthly *Victoria Magazine*, which ran from 1863 to 1880.

Emily played her part as entrepreneur well. She was described

as looking like 'a stout business gentleman', and probably con-
founded her rather high-caste peers in the literary and artistic
circles she had frequented as a young debutante in the 1850s,
particularly when she became involved in a sensational divorce
case in 1865, during which an admiral, suing for divorce, was
accused by his wife of the attempted rape of a family friend:
Emily. In true Victorian style, it was Emily who suffered most
from the accusation. On hearing of the case, Bessie Rayner Parkes's
husband dubbed her 'a dangerous woman ... of impure mind',
and a lucrative slice of any potential market for Victoria Press
publications was lost, along with Emily's own reputation.

She continued to campaign, even after relinquishing the Press in
1881, for women's gainful employment, lecturing both at home
and in the United States, and was proud of the fact that she was
one of the first *practical* feminists. 'Usefulness is the rent we are
asked to pay for room on the earth,' said her contemporary, the
educationalist Dorothea Beale, adding tartly that 'some of us are
heavily in debt'.[12] But Emily Faithfull was not one of those.

There is a final group of workers I would like to mention in this
history of spirited women, and that is the ladies of the North
American goldfields. Even though books have been written about
them,[13] there are certain individuals whose feistiness should be
honoured here. Charley Parkhurst (1812–79) for one. Like James
Barry, Charley's true sex was not discovered until after her death,
by which time she had become the first woman recorded to have
voted (in 1868, as a man) in a presidential election. She was an
orphan, who ran away from the New Hampshire workhouse in
which she had been brought up, and got a job, dressed as a lad,
in a livery stable. There she learned the business of driving horses,
and became a driver herself, first on the Eastern seaboard, then
in Georgia, and finally in California during the Gold Rush. She
worked on the Stockton to Mariposa stage-coach, a fearless and
trustworthy character, with a black patch where a horse had kicked

out her left eye, constantly chewing tobacco (she died of cancer of the tongue), and once allegedly shooting dead two highway robbers who tried to steal her costly cargo. She was a celebrated character.

There was another celebrated Charley of the old Wild West: 'Mountain Charley', also known as Mrs E. J. Guerin who, according to her autobiography, lived 'thirteen years in male attire'.[14] She operated during the 1850s not as a stage-coach driver but as the owner of a mule-pack courier service, as well as a prospector in California and near Pike's Peak in Colorado. She was also an unofficial member of the American Fur Company, trading with American Indians in Nebraska, and a saloon-keeper at some gold-mines near Denver. All this after having decided, as the lone mother of several children, to earn her living as a waiter on a riverboat and a brakesman on the Illinois Central Railroad. She was a restless soul, who yearned for – and attained – a life completely out of bounds.

That is what the gold-fields offered these salt-blooded women: a chance to be adventuresome, free of the over-cooked regulations of civilized life, and to make enormous sums of money. At one stage of her career, Mountain Charley boasted of having sent $30,000 home to her children, while another prospector, Ellie Nay, founded the Ellendale mine (named after her) in Nevada which, during 1910, yielded gold worth some $52,000.[15]

It is important not to lose sight of what 'ordinary' working women were doing at the same time as these rather more idiosyncratic ones. The 1841 population census shows 22.9 per cent of Britain's women and girls in employment – just over two million – with 75 per cent of them in domestic service, the textile industry, or agriculture.[16] In 1851 the numbers had grown to 28.9 per cent, nearly three million, and this time some 80 per cent of them were 'below stairs'. The same sort of percentage obtained until the end of the nineteenth century. But in 1867 the typewriter was invented, and gradually women started featuring in clerical jobs. In 1875 the first ladies were employed by the Post Office Savings Bank (their appointment, first mooted in 1872, was heavily opposed by male incumbents); in 1894 there were even women working in the Bank of England (only counting notes, of course, and they had to resign upon marriage).

The remaining 25 per cent of the working women and girls recorded by the 1841 census as in employment are remarkable for the diversity and reach of their careers. It was the first census to think of recording women's occupations, and is a gift for social historians. There, named, are women doing jobs that we in our ignorance are amazed at. Here we have the first *official*, and truly fascinating glimpse behind the scenes at working Englishwomen, showing them operating in an array of careers most people would consider to have been the sole province of men before the mid twentieth century:[17]

38 auctioneers
7 bankers
469 blacksmiths
19 boat- or barge-builders
110 braziers
106 bricklayers
74 builders
389 carpenters and joiners
478 carriers, carters, or waggoners
13 cattle or sheep-dealers
125 chimney sweeps
53 engineers or engine workers
2 gas fitters
51 leech-bleeders and dealers
25 lead-miners
12 manufacturing chemists
17 opticians
69 plasterers

33 stone-quarriers
2 sawyers
48 ship and smack [fishing boat] owners
11 slaters
11 spectacle-makers
9 surgical instrument makers
68 tin-miners
103 tin plate workers
72 undertakers

I have to admit, for all the abstruse and specialized careers on offer in 1841, one of my favourite census entries is perhaps the homeliest of all. It was written by Mary Sykes, aged sixty-five and head of her family in Barnsley. Under 'occupation' she has simply but bravely written 'Supported by a Mangle'.[18]

By 1898 the scope for making an honourable livelihood had widened even further. In a guide published by the newly founded Women's Institute, ladies are positively encouraged to go out into the world and try whatever they had a mind to do. Plenty of examples are forthcoming for those who needed the comfort of precedent. It is not possible to be a chartered accountant yet, advises the author of this guide, but there are some unchartered women practising on their own quite successfully. The Royal Institute of British Architects might not welcome women, but – unlike most other professional associations – it has not explicitly banned them. You can become an artificial eye-maker ('an apprenticeship has to be served, as for the first year the work of a beginner is useless'); there are many false-teeth manufacturers and some 1,340 chemists, druggists and dispensers. Several ladies are dentists, and over 50,000 are in the medical profession, either as nurses, doctors, surgeons or physicians.

There are astronomical assistants (again, the Royal Astronomical Society failed specifically to exclude women) and even a professional entomologist, working at the Royal Agricultural Society advising on insect and fungoid pests. Plenty of painters and decorators feature, including one Mrs Catherine Coombs, who supported herself for forty-three years; plenty of newspaper journalists (but no editor), and a raft of commercial travellers. Ships' pilots, baby-farm inspectors, piano-tuners, jewellers, feather-curlers and civil servants help make up the numbers, as well as all the usual things like governesses, teachers, ladies' companions, seamstresses and laundresses. In theory, and to a certain extent in practice – according to the Women's Institute – the world had at last become the working lady's oyster.[19]

So what about the so-called glass ceiling we hear so much about today? When was that erected, and by whom? It was not there when Pandora's daughters flourished in the pre-Christian Empires of ancient Greece and Rome. It would have been an irrelevance then: women in general may have been caricatured as deities, temptresses or scolds, but most of the limitations imposed on them (by men and the gods) were of a moral and abstract nature. In some cultures they were legally disadvantaged too, of course, but if certain women flourished as influential individuals, to prove exceptions to the general rule, that was acceptable. It might have been argued that ladies like Artemisia and Theano, like the Pharaoh's chief physician Merit Ptah, the chemist Tapputi-Belatekallim of Sumeria, or the alchemists of Alexandria, were all divinely ordained to succeed.

A little later on, the intellect of Trotula and of the Empress Theodora gave them immunity from the inherent frailties of their femininity. It was a God-given bonus (in the diluted spirit of the Virgin Mary's moral pre-eminence). Christine de Pizan and Hildegard of Bingen shared in this heavenly bounty, and were allowed to prosper, just as Margaret Paston, Margery Kempe, and the businesswomen Alice Chester and Joan Buckland were, although these last four were granted oblique permission to do so by their husbands (alive or dead).

The end of the medieval period saw the first hints of a woman

[177]

being expected to know her place. Those instruction books telling women to stay at home to avoid appearing at large as 'strumpets and gigggelots', and what their domestic duties were as virtuous daughters and wives – together with the first written articulation in England of their legal rights in *The Lawes Resolutions* – presaged the limitations of the Age of Reason. Exemption was allowed for the exigencies of the Civil War in England, the French Revolution, and the War of Independence in America. But increasingly, what was expected of a woman was more and more clearly defined as the seventeenth and eighteenth centuries progressed. So unfulfilled characters could counterfeit their sex – or forfeit it altogether. Moll Cutpurse comes to mind, and the pirates Ann Bonny and Mary Read, the quack Sarah Mapp, who assumed the personality of 'Crazy Sally', and even Aphra Behn, living in Flanders (and possibly Sumatra) under false pretences, as a spy.

There was such a thing as polite society by now, and eccentric women were subversive of that society. The Duchess of Newcastle was unequivocal in her defence of those of her sex supposed to aspire to nothing more than 'barren brains and fruitful wombs'. The petticoteries did their best, and reformers like Bathsua Makin, Anna van Schurman, and Marys Astell, Ward and Wollstonecraft, were passionate in their pleas to, and on behalf of, people who like them needed more from life than a struggle to fit more or less comfortably into a pigeon-hole.

Meanwhile, in the plebeian background, the plasterers and glaziers and blacksmiths got on with their work.

Demographic changes made it imperative for more and more women to start making an honourable living as the nineteenth century loomed. In turn this meant that those areas in which they might earn their bread with approbation became tightly circumscribed. The concept of a working woman knowing her place gained currency, with a corresponding upsurge in counterfeit again. This was the age of the female soldiers, sailors and surgeons, who refused to surrender to a suitable occupation for a lady.

It was the age of those perceived to be intellectual freaks, too, like Caroline Herschel and Mary Anning, whose supra-feminine achievements set them apart.

As that most oppressive of centuries progressed, maverick career women became increasingly 'ungentle', until the implication was that they were not only trangressing their physical boundaries, but – like Lola Montez, Pearl Hart and Annie Newport Royall – their moral duties too. So many of the supposed virtues of the Victorian age suppressed women's independence. Even those censuses I found so refreshing only tell a small part of the story, for they only record that fraction of women recognized as working for a living. The rest, mostly members of the newly categorized middle classes, might have been desperate to work, but were disallowed by virtue of their 'breeding'. Florence Nightingale, writing in 1846, was well aware of the bitter frustration such an attitude could cause:

> What have I done this last fortnight? I have read the *Daughter at Home* to father, and two chapters of *Mackintosh*; a volume of *Sybil* to Mama. Learnt seven tunes by heart, written various letters. Ridden with Papa. Paid eight visits. Done company. And that is all . . . For how many years I have watched the drawing-room clock and thought it would never reach the ten! And twenty or thirty years more to do thus![20]

> . . . Why have women passion, intellect, moral activity – these three – and a place in society where no one of the three can be exercised? . . . In the conventional society, which men have made for women, and women have accepted, they must act the farce of hypocrisy, the lie that they are without passion – and therefore what else can they say to their daughters, without giving the lie to themselves?[21]

[179]

Nightingale rejected the lie, of course. But not all were as extraordinary as she. So-called 'distressed gentlewomen' were confined to the nursery or the schoolroom, to comforting the sick, or accompanying slightly less distressed ladies on their travels or in their homes. They tolerated their fate for lack of the confidence and conviction to challenge it. The more active men became in society (and this was the hyperactive age of imperialist and industrial expansion), the more passive women were expected to be. The right sort of women, anyway. 'Work which [is] a man's honour [is] a slur upon a woman,' noted one Victorian social historian of her age:[22] if she must find a job, simply because there is no other means of support for her, a lady has a duty to ensure that whatever she does must never threaten a man's career. In a perfect world it might be woman's fancy to find employment, but it's a man's *right*. And that is what the glass ceiling is for: to protect that right, as well as to protect the soft and milky rabble from hardening or going sour.

Come 1918, after four years of war (and all the opportunities for work – or job-sitting – it offered women), female voices were heard in the democratic process in England for the first time. And the modern age marched on, and marches yet, with women doing more and more in the workplace, and bumping their heads harder and harder on the glass, strengthened as it is now with a crust of issues regarding equal pay, working motherhood, the right (ironically) to stay at home and bring up the children, and the need, *still*, for women with careers and authority to be taken seriously.

Whenever I give lectures or workshops on Pandora's daughters, I ask whether any women listening have first-hand experience of being denied what they really wanted to do because of their sex. And always, always, there are those who respond with sometimes heartbreaking tales of thwarted ambitions and embittered working lives. And when they find themselves with the time, the confidence and the urge to explore a career, they are told they're too old.

[180]

There are articles in our local paper every now and again featuring some girl who has just managed to get a degree in mechanical engineering, or another who has become a brick-layer or fighter-pilot or train-driver. The national papers profile women captains of industry and astronauts and bankers, wondering whether they function in their families as well as they do at work (and doubting it). I often wonder whether much has changed at all.

If it has not, then in one way, I'm glad. Because if the sort of spirit that has driven all these women in the past – publicly and privately – has survived this over-regulated age and can still flourish, we should be grateful. It is an enriching spirit, a heartening one, and quite irrepressible. And I beg to differ from one who possessed it herself – Florence Nightingale – when she reckoned it so exceptional:

> Widowhood, ill-health, or want of bread, these three are supposed to justify a woman taking up an occupation. In some cases, no doubt, an indomitable force of character will suffice . . . but such are rare.[23]

Don't you believe it.

NOTES AND REFERENCES

References are given in abbreviated form in the Notes. For full details please see the Bibliography.

Introduction

1. Alfred, Lord Tennyson, *The Princess* (1847), VI, lines 290–1.
2. Sarah Mytton Maury, *An Englishwoman in America* (1848), p. 7.
3. Jane Austen, *Northanger Abbey* (1818), vol. 1, chap. 14.
4. See Jane Robinson, *Wayward Women* and *Unsuitable for Ladies*, for as stout a refutation of this image as I could manage.

1: Pandora's Daughters

1. This is according to Isodore of Seville (*c*.570–636); see Alcuin Blamires (ed.), *Woman Defamed and Woman Defended*, p. 43. © Alcuin Blamires 1992, reprinted by permission of Oxford University Press.
2. Bishop Marbod of Rennes (*c*.1035–1123); from *The Femme Fatale*, verse 1 (trans. Alcuin Blamires, op. cit., p. 100).
3. Ovid (43 BC–AD 18); from *Amores*, II, line 12 (tr. Peter Green) in *Ovid: The Erotic Poems* (Penguin, 1982).
4. Translated from the Latin Vulgate (Belfast, 1852 edition).
5. See Blamires, op. cit., p. 17.
6. There are many more or less portentous versions of Pandora's story. I first met her in the 'Wonder' section of Arthur Mee's *Children's Encyclopaedia* (1926, vol. 7, p. 4757), sandwiched between articles on photography ('The Great Miracle That Happens In The Little Black Box') and biology ('Why Are There Some Illnesses That We Cannot Get Twice?'). There she appears both glamorous and frail: an irresistible combination to an unglamorously robust eight-year-old.
7. Hesiod, *Theogony; Works and Days* (tr. Dorothea Wender), pp. 590–3.

8. Cheryl Evans (ed.), *Usborne Book of Greek and Norse Legends*, p. 36.
9. Margaret Alic, *Hypatia's Heritage*, p. 20.
10. Caroline Herzenberg, *Women Scientists from Antiquity to the Present*, p. xii.
11. Herodotus, *The Histories* (tr. G. Rawlinson), bks 7–8.
12. A trireme was the ultimate battleship, powered by three ranks of rowers – perhaps sixty oarsmen in all.
13. This and the following quotations relating to Artemisia are all from Herodotus, op. cit., pp. 540–637.
14. See Ulrike Klausmann *et al.*, *Women Pirates*, p. 81.
15. Reported to be a feature of Taoist China by Alic, op. cit., p. 47.
16. Herzenberg, op. cit., p. xii.
17. Piccione, *Excursis III: The Status of Women in Ancient Egyptian Society*, p. 4.
18. Noted in Herzenberg, op. cit., p. xv; Pythias of Assos (384–322 BC) is supposed to have collaborated with her husband (on their honeymoon!) in writing an Encyclopaedia of Botany, Biology and Physiology . . .
19. See Alic, op. cit., p. 37.
20. This account of Hypatia's death is a loose translation of that of fifth-century scholar, Socrates Scholasticus, who had her razed with 'sharp shells'; Edward Gibbon in *The . . . Decline and Fall of the Roman Empire* (1776–88) substituted shards of pottery for the shells, while the Protestant commentator John Toland (1720) decided that Hypatia – 'most beautiful, most virtuous, most learned and in every way accomplished' – was torn to pieces by the frenzied monks without any need for tools at all.
21. St Fabiola (died *c*.399) was a wealthy Roman matron commemorated for her scholarship (being proficient in Greek and Hebrew), her thirst for spiritual self-improvement (basing herself in Bethlehem at one stage as a disciple of St Jerome), and most of all for the hospital she established with her friend Paula. This hospital was designed not only to shelter travellers (the original meaning of the word) but as the first large institution to care for and even cure the sick. According to some accounts Fabiola may have practised there herself as surgeon and nurse.
22. See Jane Robinson, *Wayward Women*, p. 157.

23. There was no chance of being a good woman, of course, unless one belonged to one of these three estates.
24. See Peter Stanford, *The She-Pope: A Quest for . . . Pope Joan*, p. 64.
25. The principal sources for my treatment of Joan's story are Joan Morris, *Pope John VIII*; Rosemary and Darroll Pardoe, *The Female Pope*; and Peter Stanford, *The She-Pope*. See the general bibliography for further details and references.
26. Elizabeth Mason-Hohl, *Trotula of Salerno: The Diseases of Women*, pp. 1–2.
27. Blamires, op. cit., p. 51; from *The Appearance of Women* (tr. C. W. Marx, 1992).
28. Mid thirteenth century; now held in St John's College Library, Cambridge: MS K.26 f.4r.

2: Far Above Rubies

1. Christine de Pizan, *Book of the City of Ladies* (tr. R. Brown-Grant), p. 7.
2. Noted by Jacques Delarum in Duby and Perrot (eds.), *A History of Women in the West*, vol. 2, p. 41.
3. The opening lines of *The Good Woman* (tr. C. W. Marx. 1992). See Alcuin Blamires, *Woman Defamed and Woman Defended*, p. 228.
4. From Marbod of Rennes, *The Femme Fatale*, verse 3 (tr. Blamires, op. cit., p. 101).
5. From Anon., *The Life of Secundus*: 'What is Woman?' (tr. Blamires, op. cit., p. 100).
6. See St Thomas Aquinas, *Summa Theologiae* (tr. Edmund Hill), p. 35.
7. Jean de Meun, *The Romance of the Rose* (tr. J. Robinson), lines 9903–11.
8. Proverbs 31: 11–31.
9. *fl.* twelfth century BC; see Judges 4–5.
10. See Sheila Lewenhak, *Women and Work*, p. 127. Also Acts 16.14–15.
11. Hildegard's work includes three books of visions: *Scio vias domini* (*Know the Ways of God*, 1151), *Liber vitae meritorium* (*The Book of Life's Merits*, 1162), and *Liber divinorum operum* (*The Book*

of Divine Works, 1174); also *Physica* (an encyclopaedia of natural history) and the medical treatise *Causa et Curae*, these last two originally published together between 1150 and 1160.

12. From Hildegard of Bingen, *Causa et Curae*, quoted in Andrea Hopkins, *Most Wise and Valiant Ladies*, pp. 99–100.
13. Quoted in Blamires, op. cit., p. 167.
14. Translated by the author from the Paston Letters in the British Library (MS Add.34889 ff.36–37).
15. Ibid., (MS Add.34888 f.29).
16. In thirteenth-century Paris, there were no fewer than fifteen all-women guilds, usually to do with textiles; in London many of the guilds were mixed, and a merchant's wife (not necessarily his widow, even) was allowed to operate independently within her guild as a 'femme sole', providing her business was in a completely different line from her husband's.
17. See David Herlihy, *Opera Muliebra: Women and Work in Medieval Europe*, p. 77.
18. Carol Adams, *From Workshop to Warfare*, p. 29.
19. Vicki Leon, *Uppity Women of Medieval Times*, p. 119.
20. Adams, op. cit., p. 29.
21. Documented in Margaret Wade Labarge, *A Small Sound . . . Women in Medieval Life*, p. 160.
22. Ibid., p. 151.
23. Anastasia is sometimes mooted as a possible illustrator of Christine de Pizan's Collected Works (MS Harley 4431, British Library): see Charity Cannon Willard, *Christine de Pizan*, p. 85.
24. Caroline Barron and Anne Sutton (eds), *Medieval London Widows 1300–1500*, p. 99.
25. Ibid., p. 113.
26. See E. Carus-Wilson, *Medieval Merchant Venturers*, p. 93; Sheila Lewenhak, *Women and Work*, p. 128.
27. Sally Fox (ed.), *The Medieval Woman: An Illuminated Book of Days*.
28. Pizan, *Book of the City of Ladies* op. cit., p. 141.
29. See A. Vigier (tr.) *Christine de Pizan*, pp. 59–66.
30. Ibid., p. 77. *Le Livre de la Mutation* is translated by Vigier.
31. Pizan, *City of Ladies* op. cit., p. 6.
32. Ibid., p. 6.
33. Ibid., p. 239.

34. See Vigier, op. cit., p. xix.
35. The complete *Book of Margery Kempe* was lost, only emerging from a private collection in 1934, still in the original fifteenth-century manuscript.
36. *The Book of Margery Kempe* (trans. B. A. Windeatt), p. 45.
37. Leon, op. cit., p. 10.
38. *Printing History 18*, vol. 9, no. 2 (1987), pp. 5–12; Anne Laurence, *Women in England 1500–1760*, p. 175.
39. Emilie Amt (ed.), *Women's Lives in Medieval Europe*, p. 199.
40. Vicki Leon, *Uppity Women of the Renaissance*, p. 12.
41. Dame Juliana Berners (or Barnes), born *c.*1388; said to be an Essex woman who became Prioress of Sopwell Nunnery in Hertfordshire, who meanwhile enjoyed and excelled at the 'innocent diversions' about which she wrote. See *Dictionary of National Biography* and Barbara Gates, *Kindred Nature*, for more information.
42. An excellent modern collection of Laura's letters has been transcribed, translated and edited by Diana Robin (see Bibliography).
43. *Laura Cereta* (tr. D. Robin), pp. 78–9.
44. Frances and Joseph Gies, *Women in the Middle Ages*, p. 96.
45. Lewenhak, op. cit., p. 106.
46. Elise Boulding,*The Underside of History*, p. 494.
47. Labarge, op. cit., p. 207.
48. Amt, op. cit., p. 108.
49. Margaret Nicholas, *The World's Wickedest Women*, p. 152.
50. There are many biographical accounts of Mother Shipton, ranging from 1641 (the first dated edition) to the most recent, Jon Easton's *English Prophets: Mother Shipton*. I have used the latter, with a chapbook edition of *c.*1740, for my treatment of her story.
51. See Easton, op. cit., p. 3 (quoting from the 1641 edition).
52. It must be said that no one seems quite sure when organized publication of Mother Shipton's *Prophecies* began . . .
53. *Notes and Queries*, vol. 9 (1872), p. 451.

3: *Madde Pranckes and Merry Molls*

1. T. Middleton and T. Dekker, *The Roaring Girle*, Act V, Sc. 1, l.333.
2. See Agnes Strickland, *Lives of the Queens of England*, vol. 2, p. 178.

3. Antonia Fraser, *The Weaker Vessel*, p. 222; S. Davies, *Unbridled Spirits*, p. 21. The identity of this 'she-soldier' is supposed to be a pregnant woman who fought under the name of 'Mr. Clarke'.
4. Fraser, op. cit., p. 221.
5. Ibid., p. 209.
6. Vicki Leon, *Uppity Women of the Renaissance*, p. 64; Fraser, op. cit., p. 228.
7. See Davies, op. cit., for a study of women dissenters.
8. The Diggers were so called because they declared themselves committed to the (metaphorical) digging of untilled land: the social and political cultivation of those people denied a voice in Royalist parliament. Levellers warned that the meek (i.e. England's poor) really would inherit the earth, toppling the avaricious rich in the name of their 'Head Leveller', Jesus Christ. Millenarians, one of whose most prominent spokeswomen was the prophetess Joanna Southcott (1750–1814), believed in the Messiah returning to earth for a period of 1000 years to empower the 'lower orders', and generally to turn the world upside down . . .
9. *The Lawes Resolutions of Women's Rights: or, The Lawes Provision for Woemen*, p. 6.
10. Olwen Hufton, *The Prospect Before Her: A History of Women in Western Europe*, vol. 1, p. 170.
11. C. J. S. Thompson, *The Quacks of Old London*, p. 274.
12. See Margaret Wade Labarge, *A Small Sound . . . Women in Medieval Life*, p. 171.
13. Thompson, op. cit., p. 147.
14. Ibid., p. 146.
15. Ivy Pinchbeck, *Women Workers and the Industrial Revolution 1750–1850*, p. 302.
16. *Gentleman's Magazine*, April 1738, p. 218.
17. *London Gazette*, June 1739, pp. 298–9.
18. Quoted in Eric Jameson, *The Natural History of Quackery*, p. 167.
19. Thompson, op. cit., p. 300.
20. I have been unable to trace this play, only coming up with an earlier effort called *The Wife's Relief, or the Husband's Cure* by Charles Johnson (1712); this ballad is quoted in C. J. S. Thompson's invaluable *Quacks of Old London*, p. 302.
21. Potts himself was a *qualified* bone-setter as well as one of the most eminent surgeons of the day; he published a very technical

treatise 'Of Dislocations' in his *Observations on the Nature and Consequence . . . of Injuries . . .*, in 1768.

22. *The Female Jester; or, Wit for the Ladies* (London, 1778), p. 31.
23. Sadly, the *Daily Courant* was only published by Elizabeth for seven issues, even though it continued until June 1735; it is credited in Griffiths's *Encyclopaedia* with being England's first daily paper.
24. Julia Cherry Spruill, *Women's Life and Work in the Southern Colonies*, p. 288.
25. Barbara Mayer Wertheimer, *We Were There: The Story of Working Women in America*, p. 13.
26. Collated in Spruill, op. cit.
27. Fraser, op. cit., p. 381.
28. Alice Clark, *Working Life of Women in the Seventeenth Century*, p. 32.
29. Ulrike Klausmann *et al.*, *Women Pirates*, pp. 14–16.
30. Most notably in William Hogarth's etching *The Company of Undertakers* (1736), where she sits resplendent and grotesque in the company of celebrated 'Quack-Heads' and 'Demi-Doctors'.
31. Elise Boulding, in her book of the same name published in 1992.
32. *Newgate Calendar*, vol. 2, p. 21.
33. Ibid., p. 25.
34. From *The Tryals of Captain John Rackam*, a copy of which I can locate nowhere; quoted in Margaret Creighton and Lisa Norling (eds), *Iron Men, Wooden Women: Gender and Seafaring . . . 1700–1920*, p. 7.
35. Scholars are *almost* sure the book is by Defoe, even though the author's name on the title-page is given as Captain Charles Johnson.
36. This and the following quotations relating to Mary and Ann are all taken from [Daniel Defoe], *General History of the Robberies and Murders of the most notorious Pyrates . . .*, pp. 79–91.
37. David Jones, *Women Warriors*, p. 218.
38. I have based my account of Moll's life on her own, first appearing in *The Life and Death of Mrs Mary Frith, commonly called Moll Cutpurse* in 1662.
39. Mary Frith, *The Life and Death of . . . Moll Cutpurse*, p. 22.
40. Ibid., p. 97.
41. This is how an early biographer of Behn, 'A Gentlewoman of her Acquaintance', characterizes her leave-taking, in *The Histories and*

Novels of the Late Ingenious Mrs Behn . . . Together with The Life and Memoirs . . . (1696).

42. Honoré d'Urfé's *L'Astrée*, 1607–28.
43. Aphra's reports can still be perused today, in their entirety, in London's Public Record Office (Williamson's State Papers SO 29).
44. See Jacqueline Pearson, *The Prostituted Muse . . .*, p. 9. Male critics commonly imprecated female dramatists like Behn with accusations of intellectual harlotry, implying a corresponding laxity, of course, in morality and sexual continence.

4: *Petticoteries*

1. *Letters and Poems in Honour of . . . Margaret, Dutchess of Newcastle*, p. 162.
2. 1770 Statute against the Perfidy of Women (George III).
3. *Letters and Poems . . .* op. cit., pp. 166–7.
4. Ibid. (in an Elegy by Thomas Shadwell).
5. 'Bon ton' was a term which encompassed all that was most stylish in good breeding, fine taste and high fashion.
6. One Mr Benjamin Stillingfleet, a botanist, who rarely clothed his calves in anything else (see Anne Mountfield, *Women and Education*, p. 16).
7. Molière (1622–73) satirized the more pretentious variety of Blue-stocking – or *Bas bleu* – in his vastly popular plays *Les Précieuses Ridicules* (1659) and *Les Femmes Savantes* (1672).
8. Malebranche, Father [Nicholas], *His Treatise* (1700), p. 54. Quoted in Patricia Phillips, *The Scientific Lady . . . 1520–1918*, p. 14.
9. See the Preface to de Gournay's edition of Montaigne's *Essays* (tr. Richard Hillman and Colette Quesnel; Arizona Press, 1998).
10. Quoted in Antonia Fraser, *The Weaker Vessel*, 1984, (Amazon) p. 370.
11. *The Female Spectator* 10, pp. 205–6.
12. Lady Mary Wortley Montagu, *Works*, vol. III, pp. 87–8; see also Jane Robinson, *Wayward Women*, p. 32.
13. *Gentleman's Magazine*, October 1739, p. 525.
14. For a full discussion of the impact of the Industrial Revolution on working women, see Ivy Pinchbeck, *Women Workers and the Industrial Revolution 1750–1850*.

15. Elizabeth Sanderson, *Women and Work in Eighteenth-century Edinburgh*.

16. Namely, Thomas Orwin, *Boke His Surfeit in Love, with a farewel to the folies of his own phantasie* (1588).

17. From Jane Anger's Introduction to *Her Protection for Women* (1589), reprinted in S. O'Malley (ed.) *The Early Modern Englishwoman*, vol. 4.

18. Mary Astell, *A Serious Proposal to the Ladies*, p. 141.

19. Ibid., p. 178.

20. Quoted in Fraser, op. cit., p. 139.

21. Mary was dubbed thus by her friend Mary Poyntz whose early biography of Ward is extensively cited in Margaret Littlehales, *Mary Ward*.

22. According to Bathsua's biographer Frances Teague, her father was a schoolmaster named Henry Reginald; while other scholars have Bathsua as the sister of the mathematician John Pell, I think Teague's theory of her family history more likely. See Teague, *Bathsua Makin* (Introduction).

23. Simon D'Ewes, cited in Teague, op. cit., p. 31.

24. Bathsua Makin, *An Essay to Revive the Antient Education of Gentlewomen . . .*, pp. 3, 23.

25. Ibid., pp. 42–3.

26. Hannah Woolley, *The Gentlewoman's Companion*, p. 75.

27. Ibid., p. 167. The recipe is easy to follow:

    First, wet your paste with Butter, and cold water, roul it very thin, then lay Apples in lays and between every lay of Apples strew some fine Sugar, and some Lemon-peel cut very small; you may also put some Fennel-seed to them, let them bake an hour or more, then ice them with Rosewater, Sugar, and butter beaten together, and wash them over with the same, strew more fine Sugar over them, and put them into the Oven again; this done, you may serve them hot or cold.

    I use ready-made puff-pastry for the 'paste', cinnamon for the fennel, and probably don't strew the sugar quite as liberally as Hannah would. It's *very* delicious.

28. Ibid., p. 67.

29. An over-sentimental confection called *Mary, A Fiction* (1788).

30. Mary was bewildered and appalled by post-revolutionary France's refusal to admit women, electorally, to the new democracy. It had not happened in America either (see note 31), and despite a long and increasingly vociferous tradition of women petitioners and organized protesters, both in Britain (especially during the Civil War) and in France, it depressed her greatly to realize that women were still far from achieving their social and political rights.

31. Abigail Adams (1744–1818), wife of America's second President and mother of its sixth, was assiduous in trying to include women – or 'the ladies', as she put it – amongst those protected and empowered by the Declaration of Independence. Extracts from her correspondence with her husband show how strongly she felt:

31 March, 1776. [I]n the new code of laws which I suppose it will be necessary for you to make, I desire you would remember the ladies and be more generous and favourable to them than your ancestors. Do not put such unlimited power into the hands of the husbands. Remember, all men would be tyrants if they could. If particular care and attention is not paid to the ladies, we are determined to foment a rebellion, and will not hold ourselves bound by any laws in which we have no voice or representation . . .

Quoted in Miriam Schneir, *The Vintage Book of Historical Feminism*, p. 3.

32. Mary Wollstonecraft, *A Vindication of the Rights of Woman* (ed. Brody), pp. 121, 319, 121–2.

5: Up and Doing

1. Mary Wollstonecraft, *A Vindication of the Rights of Woman* (ed. Brody), p. 262.
2. Alexander Pope, *The Dunciad* (1728), II, lines 153–4.
3. For sixteen years Sarah Biffin (1784–1850) put herself under the 'protection' of – or essentially sold herself to – one Mr Dukes, who features in handbills advertising her shows. He used to parade her around the country with a booth in which she would sit and paint, or sign her autograph. He charged three guineas for her miniatures on ivory, but only paid Sarah five pounds a year. She was then

taken up by members of the British aristocracy, who engaged an art tutor for her, and supported her in her efforts to live by her painting. In 1821 she was awarded a medal by the Society of Artists in recognition of her talent. But as she grew older, it became increasingly difficult for her to paint, and she died in Liverpool at the age of sixty-six in near poverty (*Dictionary of National Biography*).

4. Verena Neuburger, *Margery Kempe*, p. 142.

5. See Mrs Philipps *et al.*, *Dictionary of Employments Open to Women*, p. 15.

6. There are many accounts (and legends) of women who disguised themselves as sailors and soldiers. British eighteenth-century balladry is full of distraught maids who have been wronged and run away to sea, or lusty ladies so enamoured of their mates that they follow them to the battlefields. Not just sailors and soldiers, either: there is a story about Mary Lacey, a shipwright in Portsmouth in the 1770s; several about the betrousered 'Long Meg of Westminster', publican and renowned duellist; and any amount about confused women wandering about the place in men's clothes and so encouraging the advances of male and female alike . . . I have tried to limit myself to those characters whose lives can be authenticated (except, perhaps, in the case of Mary Talbot). See Dianne Dugaw, *Warrior Women and Popular Balladry 1650–1850*; Margaret Spufford, *Small Books and Pleasant Histories*; Suzanne J. Stark, *Female Tars*; E. Vizetelly, *The Warrior Woman*; and Julie Wheelwright, *Amazons and Military Maids* for a wider picture.

7. [Christian Cavanagh], *The Life and Adventures of Mrs Christian Davies, the British Amazon, commonly called Mother Ross. Taken from her own mouth when a Pensioner at Chelsea Hospital, and Known to be True . . .*

8. Ibid., p. 20.

9. How did she – and other women disguised like her – deal with menstruation? Of course they never tell us themselves, but Snell's biographer, Matthew Stephens, makes the point that menses may have been taken for a symptom of venereal disease. One Catherine Vinken on trial (for impropriety?) in 1721 is noted in *The Tradition of Female Transvestism* (ed. B. Eriksson; London, 1989), as having used a leather dildo through which to urinate (p. 16), and as washing was a rare and unwelcome task, full nudity would not

[193]

have posed a danger. I still cannot help wondering how they coped, though.

10. Cavanagh, op. cit., p. 47.
11. Matthew Stephens in *Hannah Snell: The Secret Life of a Female Marine, 1723–1792.*
12. Charles Dickens, *All the Year Round*, 6 April 1872, p. 448.
13. Snell's story may be muddled and spuriously embellished, but appears in essence to be true. Visit the Museum of the Royal Marines at Portsmouth for more information, and for illustrations of her in all her nautical glory.
14. Published in London by R. Walker, and bearing a notice to the public assuring Hannah's trustworthiness, witnessed by the Mayor of London, Hannah's sister Susannah, and Hannah herself (with a cross).
15. Stephens, op. cit., p. 49.
16. *London Evening Post*, 5–7 July 1750.
17. Quoted by Dickens, op. cit.
18. I must admit that Talbot's account may well be fanciful (to a greater or lesser extent): no one has been able to place her as 'John Taylor' aboard any of the vessels she lists. I maintain that Mary was still an enterprising woman: had she lived, the tale would have made her money. And her contemporaries certainly believed it. See Julie Wheelwright, *Amazons and Military Maids*, p. 142–6.
19. William Hone, *The Year Book of Daily Recreation*, p. 212.
20. The title of a book about Hester by David Shore. See also S. Raven and A. Weir, *Women in History*.
21. Eliza's book was reprinted in 1925, with notes, by E. M. Forster.
22. See Jane Robinson, *Wayward Women: A Guide to Women Travellers*, p. 177.
23. From the title-page to the 1802 edition of Mariana Starke's *Letters from Italy*.
24. First published in 1857; see Robinson, op. cit., p. 270.
25. By Terry Sullivan, 1908, quoted in Crispin Tickell, *Mary Anning of Lyme Regis*, p. 26.
26. Gideon Mantell, quoted in H. Torrens, *Mary Anning*, p. 268.
27. Lady Silvester, quoted in Tickell, op. cit., p. 12.
28. Torrens, op. cit., p. 259.
29. Anna Maria Pinney, quoted in Tickell, op. cit., p. 14.
30. Ibid., p. 27.

31. Constance Lubbock, *The Herschel Chronicle*, p. 45.
32. Ibid., p. 153.
33. *A Catalogue of 860 Stars Observed by Flamsteed, but not Included in the British Catalogue*, and *A General Index of Reference to every Observation of every Star on the above-mentioned British Catalogue* (1798).
34. Mrs John Herschel, *Memoir and Correspondence of Caroline Herschel*, p. 54.
35. Lubbock, op. cit., p. 172 (my italics).

6: *Ungentlewomen*

1. Lola Montez, *Autobiography and Lectures*, p. 3.
2. See Julia Cherry Spruill, *Women's Life and Work in the Southern Colonies*.
3. Elizabeth Anthony Dexter, *Career Women of America 1776–1840*, p. 187.
4. Spruill, op. cit., p. 308; Jane Robinson, *Parrot Pie for Breakfast: An Anthology of Women Pioneers*, p. 75.
5. The first was New Jersey; only women with more than $250 were eligible to vote (see Chambers *Biographical Dictionary of Women: A Women's Chronology*, p. 716).
6. Kate Nye-Starr, in the title of a book, *A Self-Sustaining Woman* (published in Chicago, 1888), describing her working life on the railroads as ticket-seller, clerk, telegraph-operator etc. throughout America. Kate was married, but still prided herself on her financial independence.
7. John Quincy Adams, *Memoirs* (1877), p. 321; quoted in Alice Maxwell and Marion Dunleavy, *Virago! The Story of Anne Newport Royall*, p. 262.
8. Richardson Wright, *Forgotten Ladies*, p. 169.
9. Mary Livermore, a nurse with the Union Army, reckoned there were over 400 women involved in the war as soldiers, spies, cavalrymen, musicians and so on (see Mary Livermore, *My Story of the War*). Most are unnamed, although other than the women I mention in the text, the Confederate Army spy Belle Boyd and Lieutenant Madeline Moore of the Kentucky Home Guard stand out. See also S. G. Dannet, *She Rode with the Generals*, and Julie Wheelwright, *Amazons and Military Maids*.

10. Told in her autobiography, and in a lengthy newspaper article by Frank Schneider in the Detroit *Post and Tribune*, October 1883. Sarah was also known (towards the end of her life) as Emma Seelye.
11. Schneider, op. cit., quoted in Wheelwright, op. cit., p. 21.
12. Wheelwright, op. cit, p. 22.
13. Kurt Singer, *Three Thousand Years of Espionage*, p. 18.
14. Loreta Janeta Velasquez, *The Woman in Battle*, p. 97.
15. Ibid., p. 42.
16. Ibid., pp. 124–5.
17. David Jones, *Women Warriors*, p. 236.
18. Ménie Muriel Dowie, *Women Adventurers*, p. 51.
19. See Duncan Aikman, *Calamity Jane and the Lady Wildcats*.
20. Where was the Wild West, exactly? It shifted: it was the area beyond civilized settlement. And as civilized settlement reached further and further west as the nineteenth century progressed – and further and further east from the California coast, eventually – its limits grew increasingly defined to encompass what is now known as the Mid-west.
21. All three mentioned in Aikman, op. cit.
22. My sources for Starr's biography are principally James Horan, *Desperate Women*, p. 201, and Cameron Rogers, *Gallant Ladies*, p. 115 (the two titles illustrating nicely what each author thinks of Mrs Starr's exploits!).
23. I would suggest *c*.1875, which would make her about eighteen when she joined the Wild West Show in Chicago in 1893, shortly after having abandoned her husband (whom she married at sixteen) and her child. See Frances Laurence, *Maverick Women*, p. 133.
24. See Isobel Rae, *The Strange Story of Dr. James Barry*, and June Rose, *The Perfect Gentleman: The Remarkable Life of Dr James Miranda Barry*.
25. Rose, op. cit., p. 20.
26. From a letter written to Nightingale's great-nephew Sir Harry Verney, quoted in Elizabeth Longford, *Eminent Victorian Women*, p. 245.
27. During 'James''s illness in the Windward and Leeward Islands, her own assistant surgeon is said to have stolen into her room, with a friend for moral support, and eased back the bedclothes to check his suspicions, exclaiming triumphantly 'See, Barry is a woman!'

(Longford, op. cit., p. 242). Both he and the friend were sworn to secrecy. Presumably Somerset knew, too . . .

28. Rose, op. cit., p. 13.
29. See note 26.
30. Mary Seacole, *Wonderful Adventures of Mrs Seacole in Many Lands*, p. 91.
31. Emily Eden, the Governor-General of Bengal's sister, noted presciently in 1839: 'She is very pretty, and a good little thing, apparently, but [the Jameses] are very poor, and she is very young and lively, and if she falls into bad hands, she would soon laugh herself into foolish scrapes . . .' (Emily Eden, *Up the Country*, p. 341).
32. Bruce Seymour, *Lola Montez: A Life*, p. 34.
33. Montez, op. cit., p. 3.

7: Owning Oneself

1. Tennessee Claflin interviewed by Thomas Masterson, *New York Herald*, 22 January 1870.
2. 'Why Are Women Redundant?', in *National Review* 14 (1862), p. 434.
3. Anne Mountfield, *Women and Education*, p. 35.
4. Voting rights had been granted to certain women in certain states of America before this; notably to the prosperous ladies (worth $250 or more) of New Jersey in 1776, and in 1870 to the women of Utah. The dates quoted in the text refer to equal voting rights (with men) in New Zealand and America, but in Britain only women over thirty were allowed to vote until equality was achieved in 1928.
5. See Frances Power Cobbe's article in *Frasers Magazine* 66 (1862), 'What shall we do with our Old Maids?' p. 594.
6. *Punch* 18 (1850), p. 1.
7. In 1862 there were reported to be 3 per cent more females than males in Great Britain: an extra three-quarters of a million (from 'Why Are Women Redundant?' note 2 above). By 1871 the figure had grown to well over a million. There were more 'surplus' women in England at this time than in any other European state (from Edward Watherston's paper *The Industrial Employment of Women . . .*, 1878).
8. See Jane Robinson, *Parrot Pie for Breakfast*.
9. This association was set up in Lowell, Massachusetts, in 1845,

supported by the periodicals the *Lowell Offering* and the *Voice of Industry*, giving women weavers labour news and encouragement. The Association's success was largely attributable to the zeal and hard work of mill-worker Sarah G. Bagley, who later went on to become America's first woman telegrapher (Madeleine Stern, *We the Women*, p. 79).

In Britain, working hours were limited to twelve a day (for women textile workers and children over thirteen) by the Factory Act of 1844, and to fifty-eight a week by 1847.

10. The catalogue is usefully abstracted by Deborah J. Warner in Martha Moore Trescott (ed.), *Dynamos and Virgins Revisited: Women and Technological Change in History*, p. 110.

11. William Hutton, *A History of Birmingham*, p. 116. William Hutton's remarks on women smiths and nailers appeared in the 1740s; Jane Rendall in *Women in an Industrialising Society* reproduces an illustration of the 1860s showing a girl hammering nails in just the same way as Hutton witnessed a century earlier.

12. An Act was passed in 1842, after a shocking commission of inquiry, to prohibit women and children from working down the pits under any circumstances. See Ivy Pinchbeck, *Women Workers and the Industrial Revolution 1750–1850*, p. 240.

13. John Plummer (27 August 1864), quoted in Michael Hiley, *Victorian Working Women*, p. 50.

14. Hiley, op. cit., p. 50.

15. Ibid., p. 98.

16. Caroline Chisholm, *Emigration and Transportation*, p. 17: 'If Her Majesty's Government be really desirous of seeing a well-conducted community spring up in [the] Colonies, the social wants of the people must be considered . . . For all the clergy you can despatch, all the schoolmasters you can appoint, all the churches you can build, and all the books you can export, will never do much without what a gentleman in [Australia] very appropriately called "God's Police" – good and virtuous women.'

17. Elizabeth Longford, *Victoria R.I.*, p. 208; Vivien Allen, *Lady Trader: A Biography of Mrs Sarah Heckford*, p. 49.

18. Mary Reibey's letters are held by the Mitchell Library in Sydney, New South Wales. This one (with others) is reproduced in Nance Irvine (ed.), *Dear Cousin: The Reibey Letters*, p. 12. Original is held in the Mitchell Library, State Library of New South Wales.

19. See Lennard Bickel, *Australia's First Lady: The Story of Elizabeth Macarthur*.

20. Lynda Adamson, *Notable Women in World History*, p. 215.

21. Sarah Heckford, *A Lady Trader in the Transvaal* (London, 1882). See Jane Robinson, *Wayward Women*, p. 46.

22. This curious fact is noted in Allen, op. cit., p. 43.

23. Sarah had already published a serious discussion of socialism in *The Life of Christ, and its bearing on the Doctrines of Communism* (London, 1873). In it she claimed that poverty 'does not consist in having but little money: it consists in wanting to do more than can be done with the money you possess' (p. 69). She knew too many poor women . . .

24. *Oxford English Dictionary*; source dated 1803.

25. This trade-card cannot have been published until after Lydia's death, since the Brooklyn Bridge was only erected in 1883, and she would have had some difficulty in answering her correspondents personally by then.

26. An advertising slogan of Lydia's, quoted in her entry in the *Encyclopaedia Britannica* online.

27. Lois Beachy Underhill, *The Woman Who Ran for President: The Many Lives of Victoria Woodhull*, p. 38.

28. Soon after the birth of her first child, while the Woodhulls were living in San Francisco, Victoria had tried a career on the stage, earning $52 a week for a six-week run. Apparently she was a 'natural', but hated the work. See Underhill, op. cit., p. 27.

8: Out of Bounds

1. George Eliot, *Felix Holt* (1866), chap. 27.

2. Virginia Woolf, *A Room of One's Own*, p. 106.

3. See Fidelis Morgan, *The Well-known Troublemaker: A Life of Charlotte Charke*. An early critic of Charlotte was somewhat dismissive of her acting talent, noting that she specialized in male roles, and that her public hardly ever saw her act as a lady. This he found rather appropriate, given her ungentle nature.

4. Bernal Diaz del Castillo, *The Discovery and Conquest of Mexico*, p. 68.

5. Quoted in an article by Shep Lenchek ('"La Malinche" – Harlot or Heroine?') in *El Ojo del Lago*, vol. 14, no. 4 (December 1997).

6. Vicki Leon, *Uppity Women of Medieval Times*, p. 8.
7. Charlotte Charke, *A Narrative of the Life*, p. 23.
8. Reprinted in Morgan, op. cit., p. 124.
9. Michael Hiley, *Victorian Working Women*, p. 119.
10. Clara True wrote an account of her working life in *The Outlook*, 5 June 1909, p. 331.
11. James Stone, *Emily Faithfull*, p. 55 (quoting from the *Women's Penny Paper*, 8 February 1890, p. 481).
12. Dorothea Beale was speaking at the Conference on Women Workers organized by the National Union of Women Workers of Great Britain and Ireland in November 1903. See National Union of Women Workers, *Papers read at the Conference . . .*, p. 59.
13. Notably Sally Zanjani, *A Mine of her Own: Women Prospectors in the American West 1850–1950*, and Jo Ann Levy, *They Saw the Elephant: Women in the California Goldrush*.
14. Mrs E. J. Guerin, *Mountain Charley or the Adventures of Mrs E. J. Guerin*, title-page.
15. Zanjani, op. cit., p. 160.
16. Statistics taken from Duncan Crow, *The Victorian Woman*, p. 71.
17. Abstracted from Ivy Pinchbeck, *Women Workers and the Industrial Revolution 1750–1850*, p. 692.
18. From the 1851 census.
19. See Mrs Philipps *et al.*, *Dictionary of Employments Open to Women* (1898).
20. From Florence Nightingale's diary, 1846, quoted in Crow, op. cit., p. 42.
21. Florence Nightingale, 'Cassandra' (in *Suggestions for Thought to the Searchers after Truth*, vol. 2), p. 396.
22. Georgiana Hill in her study *Women in English Life*, p. 185.
23. Nightingale, op. cit., p. 401.

BIBLIOGRAPHY

Abbot, W., *Notable Women in History* (Philadelphia, Penn.: Winston, 1913).

Adair, James, *Essays on Fashionable Diseases . . . And on Quacks and Quackery* (London: Bateman, c.1790).

Adams, Carol, *From Workshop to Warfare* (Cambridge: Cambridge University Press, 1990).

Adams, John Quincy, *Memoirs* (Philadelphia, Penn.: Lippincott, 1874–7).

Adamson, Lynda, *Notable Women in World History* (Westport, Conn.: Greenwood Press, 1998).

Aikman, Duncan, *Calamity Jane and the Lady Wildcats* (New York: Holt, 1927).

Alic, Margaret, *Hypatia's Heritage* (London: Women's Press, 1986).

Allen, Vivien, *Lady Trader: A Biography of Mrs Sarah Heckford* (London: Collins, 1979).

Amt, Emilie (ed.), *Women's Lives in Medieval Europe* (New York: Routledge, 1993).

Anderson, Janet, *Women in the Fine Arts: A Bibliography* (Jefferson, Tex.: McFarland, 1991).

Anger, Jane (ed. S. O'Malley), *Her Protection for Women. In The Early Modern Englishwoman*, vol. 4 (London: Ashgate, 1996).

Anon. [Allestree, Richard], *The Lady's Calling* (Oxford: for the Chancellor, 1673).

Anon. [Chudleigh, Elizabeth], *The Ladies Defence: or, the Bride-Woman's Counsellor Answer'd* (London: Deeve, 1701).

Anon., *Female Rights Vindicated; or the Equality of the Sexes Morally and Physically Proved . . . by a Lady* (London: Burnett, 1758).

Anon. [Tipper, John], *The Ladies Diary* (London: Wilde, 1708).

Anon. [attrib. Woolley, Hannah], *The Accomplish't Lady's Delight, In Preserving, Physick, Beautifying and Cookery* (London: Harris, 1675).

Anon., *The Female Jester; or, Wit for the Ladies* (London: Bew and Lewis, 1778).

Anon., *The History of Mother Shipton* (London [publisher unknown], c.1740).

Aquinas, Thomas (tr. E. Hill), *Summa Theologiae* (London: Blackfriars/Eyre and Spottiswoode, 1963).

[201]

Astell, Mary (ed. B. Hill), *A Serious Proposal to the Ladies*, parts I [1694] and II [1697], reprinted in *The First English Feminist* (Aldershot: Gower, 1986).

Austen, Jane, *Northanger Abbey* (London: Murray, 1818).

Ayscough, Florence, *Chinese Women Yesterday and Today* (Boston, Mass.: Houghton Mifflin, 1937).

Ballard, George (ed. R. Berry), *Memoirs of Several Ladies of Great Britain* [1752] (Detroit: Wayne State University Press, 1985).

Balsdon, J. P. V. D., *Roman Women* (London: Bodley Head, 1974).

Barber, M. A. S., *Bread-Winning; or The Ledger and the Lute* (London: Macintosh, 1865).

Barnes, Dame Juliana (ed. T. Satchell), *An Older Form of the Treatyse of Fysshynge with an Angle* (London: English Dialect Society, 1883).

[Barnes] Berners, Dame Juliana, *A Treatyse of Fysshynge with an Angle* [1496] (London: Stock, 1880).

Barron, Caroline and Sutton, Anne (eds), *Medieval London Widows 1300–1500* (London: Hambledon, 1994).

Barstow, Anne Llewellyn, *Witchcraze* (San Francisco, Cal.: Pandora, 1994).

Behn, Aphra, *The Histories and Novels of the Late Ingenious Mrs Behn . . . [with a memoir] by One of the Fair Sex* (London: Briscoe, 1696).

——, *Love Letters between a Nobleman and his Sister* [1684–7] (London: Virago, 1987).

——, *Oroonoko: or, the Royal Slave. A True History* (London: Canning, 1688).

——, (ed. J. Lipking). *Oroonoko* (New York: Norton, 1997).

Beik, Doris and Paul, *Flora Tristan, Utopian Feminist* (Bloomington, Ind.: Indiana University Press, 1993).

Bickel, Lennard, *Australia's First Lady: The Story of Elizabeth Macarthur* (Sydney: Allen and Unwin, 1991).

Blamires, Alcuin (ed.), *Woman Defamed and Woman Defended* (Oxford: Oxford University Press, 1992).

Boccaccio, Giovanni (tr. G. A. Guarino), *Concerning Famous Women* [*De Claris Mulieribus*] (London: Allen and Unwin, 1964).

Boulding, Elise, *The Underside of History* (Boulder, Colo.: Westview, 1976).

Brown, Dee, *The Gentle Tamers: Women of the Old Wild West* (New York: Putnam, 1958).

Burton, Sarah, *Impostors. Six Kinds of Liar* [incl. James Barry, Charley Pankhurst] (London: Viking, 2000).

Butler, Charles (ed.), *Female Replies to Swetnam the Woman-Hater* [Constantia

Munda, *The Worming of the Mad Dogge*; Esther Sowernam, *Ester hath hang'd Haman*; Rachel Speght, *A Mouzell for Melastomus*] (Bristol: Thoemmes Press, 1995).

Canning, John (ed.), *100 Great Lives of Antiquity* (London: Methuen, 1985).

Capp, Bernard, *Astrology and the Popular Press: English Almanacs 1500–1800* (New York: Faber, 1979).

Carus-Wilson, E., *Medieval Merchant Venturers* (London: Methuen, 1954).

del Castillo, Bernal Diaz (ed. G. Garcia), *The Discovery and Conquest of Mexico* (New York: Straus and Cudahy, 1956).

[Cavanagh, Christian], *The Life and Adventures of Mrs Christian Davies, the British Amazon, commonly called Mother Ross ... taken from her own mouth? when a Pensioner at Chelsea Hospital, and Known to be True ...* (London: Montagu, 1740).

Cavendish, Margaret, Duchess of Newcastle, see *Letters and Poems ...*

de Cereta, Laura (tr. D. Robin), *Collected Letters of a Renaissance Feminist* (Chicago, Ill.: University of Chicago Press, 1997).

Chambers Biographical Dictionary of Women (ed. Melanie Parry) (Edinburgh: Chambers, 1996).

Charke, Charlotte, *A Narrative of the Life* (London: Reeve, 1755).

Children's Encyclopaedia (ed. A. Mee) (London: Educational Book Company, 1926).

Chisholm, Caroline, *Emigration and Transportation* (London: Ollivier, 1847).

——, *The A.B.C. of Colonization* (London: Ollivier, 1850).

Churchill, Caryl, *Top Girls* [incl. Pope Joan] (London: French, 1982).

Claflin, Tennessee [Lady Cook], *Essays ... on the Evils of Society* (New York: Roxburghe Press, 1896).

Clark, Alice, *Working Life of Women in the Seventeenth Century* [1913] (London: Routledge, 1982).

Cobbe, Frances Power, *What Shall We Do with our Old Maids?* (*Frasers Magazine*, vol. 66; London, 1862).

Costello, Louisa, *Memoirs of Eminent Englishwomen* (London: Bentley, 1844).

Creighton, Margaret and Norling, Lisa (eds), *Iron Men, Wooden Women: Gender and Seafaring ... 1700–1920* (Baltimore, Md.: Johns Hopkins University Press, 1996).

Crow, Duncan, *The Victorian Woman* (London: Allen and Unwin, 1971).

Dannet, S. G., *She Rode with the Generals* [Sarah Edmonds] (New York: Nelson, 1960).

Davies, S., *Unbridled Spirits: Women of the English Revolution 1640–1660* (London: Women's Press, 1998).

Davis, Elizabeth Gould, *The First Sex* (London: J. M. Dent, 1973).

[Defoe, Daniel], *A General History of the Robberies and Murders of the most notorious Pyrates ... by Captain Charles Johnson* (London: Rivington, 1726).

Dexter, Elizabeth Anthony, *Career Women of America 1776–1840* (Francestown, NH: Jones, 1950).

Dowie, Ménie Muriel, *Women Adventurers* [abridged accounts of Loreta Velasquez, Hannah Snell, Mary Anne Talbot and Christian Davies/Cavanagh] (London: Fisher Unwin, 1893).

Duby, G. and Perrot, M. (general editors), *A History of Women in the West.* [1: *Ancient Goddesses to Christian Saints*; 2: *Silences of the Middle Ages*; 3: *Renaissance and Enlightenment Paradoxes*; 4: *Emerging Feminism from Revolution to World War*] (Cambridge, Mass.: Belknap Press, 1994–5).

Duffy, Maureen, *The Passionate Shepherdess: Aphra Behn 1640–1689* (London: Methuen, 1989).

Dugaw, Dianne, *Warrior Women and Popular Balladry 1650–1850* (Cambridge: Cambridge University Press, 1989).

D'Urfé, Honoré (tr. Steven Rendall), *L'Astrée* [1607–28] (Binghamton, NY: Medieval and Renaissance Texts and Studies, 1995).

Dzielska, Maria, *Hypatia of Alexandria* (Cambridge, Mass.: Harvard University Press, 1995).

Easton, Jon (ed.), *English Prophets: Mother Shipton* (Chester: Fenris, 1998).

Eden, Emily, *Up the Country* (London: Bentley, 1866).

Ellis, Peter Berresford, *Celtic Women* (London: Constable, 1995).

Europa Biographical Dictionary of British Women (ed. Anne Crawfords, Tony Hayter, Ann Hughes *et al.*) (London: Europa, 1983).

Ewart, Andrew, *The World's Wickedest Women* (London: Odhams, 1964).

Fay, Eliza (ed. E. M. Forster), *Original Letters from India 1779–1815* [1815] (London: Hogarth Press, 1925).

Field, C. W., *Distaff: Female Biography from earliest times to 1800* (Robertsbridge, Sussex: Field, 1988).

Fonte, Moderata (tr. V. Cox), *The Worth of Women* (Chicago, Ill.: University of Chicago Press, 1997).

Fox, Sally (ed.), *The Medieval Woman: An Illuminated Book of Days* (London: Collins, 1985).

Fraser, Antonia, *The Weaker Vessel: Women's Lot in Seventeenth-Century England* (London: Weidenfeld and Nicolson, 1984).

Fredeman, William, *Emily Faithfull and the Victoria Press* (London [publisher unknown], 1973).

[204]

Frith, Mary (ed. R. Nakayama), *The Life and Death of Mary Frith, commonly called Moll Cutpurse* [1662] (New York: Garland, 1993).

Gates, Barbara, *Kindred Nature: Victorian and Edwardian Women Embrace the Living World* (Chicago, Ill.: University of Chicago Press, 1998).

Gies, Frances and Joseph, *Women in the Middle Ages* (New York: Harper and Row, 1978).

Gilbert, O. P., *Women in Men's Guise* (London: John Lane, 1932).

Griffiths, D. (ed.), *The Encyclopaedia of the British Press 1422–1992* (London: Macmillan, 1992).

[Guerin, Mrs E. J.] Mazzulla, Fred and Kostka, William (eds), *Mountain Charley, or the Adventures of Mrs E.J. Guerin, who was thirteen years in male attire* [1861] (Oklahoma, Okla.: University of Oklahoma Press, 1968).

Hale, Sarah, *Lessons from Women's Lives* (Edinburgh: Nimmo, 1867).

Hall, Richard, *Patriots in Disguise* [incl. Sarah Edmonds and Loreta Velasquez] (New York: Paragon House, 1993).

Hamlyn, Matthew (ed.), *The Recipes of Hannah Woolley* (London: Heinemann Kingswood, 1988).

Harpwood, Diane, *Tea and Tranquillisers* (London: Virago, 1981).

Harrison, William H., *Mother Shipton Investigated* [1881] (London: Harrison, 1976).

Haywood, Eliza (ed. G. Firmager), *The Female Spectator* (Bristol: Bristol Classical Press, 1993).

Heckford, Sarah, *A Lady Trader in the Transvaal* (London: Sampson Low *et al.*, 1882).

——, *The Life of Christ, and its bearing on the Doctrines of Communism* (London: Field and Tuer, 1873).

Henderson, Tony, *Disorderly Women in Eighteenth-Century London* (London: Longman, 1999).

Herlihy, David, *Opera Muliebra: Women and Work in Medieval Europe* (Philadelphia, Penn.: Temple University Press, 1990).

Herodotus (tr. G. Rawlinson), *The Histories* (London: J. M. Dent, 1992).

——, (tr. W. Shepherd), *The Persian War* (Cambridge: Cambridge University Press, 1982).

Herschel, Caroline, *A Catalogue of 860 Stars Observed by Flamsteed, but not Included in the British Catalogue, and A General Index of Reference to every Observation of every Star on the above-mentioned British Catalogue* (London: Elmsly, 1798).

Herschel, Mrs John, *Memoir and Correspondence of Caroline Herschel* (London: Murray, 1876).

[205]

Herzenberg, Caroline, *Women Scientists from Antiquity to the Present* (West Cornwall: Locust Hill Press, 1986).

Hesiod (tr. D. Wender), *Theogony; Works and Days* (Harmondsworth: Penguin, 1973).

Highfill, Philip, *et al.*, *Biographical Dictionary of Actors 1660–1800* (Carbondale, Ill.: South Illinois University Press, 1975).

Hiley, Michael, *Victorian Working Women* (London: Fraser, 1979).

Hill, Christopher, *The World Turned Upside Down* (London: Temple Smith, 1972).

Hill, Georgiana, *Women in English Life* (London: Bentley, 1896).

Holcombe, Lee, *Victorian Ladies at Work* (Newton Abbot: David and Charles, 1973).

Hone, William, *The Year Book of Daily Recreation* (London: Tegg, 1832).

Hopkins, Andrea, *Most Wise and Valiant Ladies* [incl. Christine de Pizan, Hildegard of Bingen, Margery Kempe, Margaret Paston] (London: Collins and Brown, 1997).

Hopkins, James, *A Woman to Deliver Her People: A Study of Joanna Southcott and English Millenarianism* (Austin, Tex.: University of Texas Press, 1982).

Horan, James, *Desperate Women* [incl. Pearl Hart, Belle Starr] (New York: Putnam, 1952).

Hufton, Olwen, *The Prospect Before Her: A History of Women in Western Europe*, vol 1: 1500–1800 (London: Fontana, 1997).

Hutton, William, *An History of Birmingham* (Birmingham: Pearson, 1795).

Ireland, N. O., *Index to Women of the World from Ancient to Modern Times* (London: Scarecrow, 1988).

Irvine, Nance (ed.), *Dear Cousin: The Reibey Letters* (Sydney, NSW: Janet Press, 1992).

Irwin, Inez Haynes, *Angels and Amazons: A Hundred Years of American Women* (New York: Doubleday, 1933).

James, Edward, James, Janet Wilson and Boyer, Paul, *Notable American Women 1607–1950* (Cambridge, Mass.: Harvard University Press, 1971).

Jameson, Eric, *The Natural History of Quackery* (London: Michael Joseph, 1961).

Jerrold, Walter and Claire, *Five Queer Women* [incl. Eliza Haywood] (New York: Brentano's, 1929).

[Jinner, Sarah], *The Woman's Almanac* (London: Streater, 1659).

Jones, David, *Women Warriors* (Washington: Brassey's, 1997).

Kemp-Welch, Alice, *Of Six Medieval Women* [incl. Christine de Pizan] (London: Macmillan, 1913).

[206]

Kempe, Margery (tr. B. A. Windeatt), *The Book of Margery Kempe* (Harmondsworth: Penguin, 1994).

Kenyon, Olga, *800 Years of Women's Letters* (Stroud: Sutton, 1992).

Klausmann, Ulrike, Meinzerin, Marion, and Kuhn, Gabriel, *Women Pirates* (Montreal: Black Rose Press, 1997).

Knapp, Samuel, *Female Biography* (Philadelphia, Penn.: Wardle, [1834]).

Labarge, Margaret Wade, *A Small Sound . . . Women in Medieval Life* (London: Hamish Hamilton, 1986).

Lacey, Mary, *The Female Shipwright* (Hull: Clayton, *c*.1800).

Laurence, Anne, *Women in England 1500–1760* (London: Weidenfeld and Nicolson, 1994).

Laurence, Frances, *Maverick Women: Nineteenth-century Women who Kicked Over the Traces* (Carpinteria, Cal.: Manifest Press, 1998).

The Lawes Resolutions of Woman's Rights (London [Miles Flesher], 1632).

Lenihan, Edmund, *Ferocious Irish Women* [incl. Alice Kyteler] (Dublin: Mercier Press, 1991).

Leon, Vicki, *Uppity Women of Medieval Times* (Berkeley, Cal.: Conari Press, 1997).

——, *Uppity Women of the Renaissance* (Berkeley, Cal.: Conari Press, 1999).

Letters and Poems in Honour of the Incomparable Princess Margaret, Dutchess of Newcastle (London: Newcombe, 1676).

Levy, Jo Ann, *They Saw the Elephant: Women in the California Goldrush* (Hamden, Conn.: Archon, 1990).

Lewenhak, Sheila, *Women and Work* (London: Fontana, 1980).

Lewis, Jane, *Women in England 1870–1950* (Brighton, Ind.: Indiana University Press, 1984).

Littlehales, Margaret, *Mary Ward* (Tunbridge Wells: Burns and Oates, 1998).

Livermore, Mary, *My Story of the War. A Woman's Narrative of Four Years . . . as Nurse in the Union Army* (Hartford, Conn.: Worthington, 1888).

Longford, Elizabeth, *Eminent Victorian Women* (London: Weidenfeld and Nicolson, 1981).

——, *Victoria R.I.* (London: Weidenfeld and Nicolson, 1964).

Lubbock, Constance (ed.), *The Herschel Chronicle* (Cambridge: Macmillan/Cambridge University Press, 1933).

Macdonald, J. Ramsay (ed.), *Women in the Printing Trades: A Sociological Study* (London: Women's Industrial Council, 1904).

Macksey, Joan and Kenneth, *Guinness Guide to Feminine Achievements* (Enfield: Guinness, 1975).

Macmillan Dictionary of Women's Biography (ed. Jennifer Uglow), (London: Macmillan, 1982).

Makin, Bathsua, *An Essay to Revive the Antient Education of Gentlewomen . . .* (London: J.D., 1673).

Malam, John, *Mary Seacole* (London: Evans, 1999).

Malebranche, Father [Nicholas], *His Treatise* (London: Bowyer, 1700).

Mason-Hohl, E., *Trotula of Salerno: The Diseases of Women* (Los Angeles: Ward-Ritchie, 1940).

Maxwell, Alice and Dunleavy, Marion, *Virago! The Story of Anne Newport Royall* (Jefferson, Tex.: McFarland, 1985).

McAlister, Linda Lopez (ed.), *Hypatia's Daughters: 1500 Years of Women Philosophers* (Bloomington, Ind.: Indiana University Press, 1996).

McDowell, Paula, *The Women of Grub Street . . . 1678–1730* (Oxford: Clarendon Press, 1998).

McLean, Tessa, *Medieval English Gardens* [incl. Juliana of Ely] (London: Viking, 1981).

McLeod, Enid, *The Order of the Rose: The Life and Ideas of Christine de Pizan* (London: Chatto and Windus, 1976).

Maury, Sarah Mytton, *An Englishwoman in America* (London: Richardson, 1848).

Menpes, Mortimer, *War Impressions* (London: A. & C. Black, 1901).

de Meun, Jean, *Le Roman de la Rose* (Paris: Librarie Générale Française, 1992).

Middleton, T. and Dekker, T. (ed. E. Cook), *The Roaring Girle* [1611] (London: A. & C. Black, 1997).

Miles, Rosalind, *The Women's History of the World* (London: Paladin, 1989).

Mill, John Stuart, *The Subjection of Women* (London: Longman, Green, 1869).

Montez, Lola, *Autobiography and Lectures* (London: Jones and Blackwood, 1860).

Moore, Patrick, *Caroline Herschel* (Oxford: Museum of the History of Science, 1988).

Moorhouse, Ruth and Randall, Chris, *Herstory: The Life of Phoebe Hessel* (Brighton: QueenSpark Books, 1994).

Morgan, Fidelis, *The Well-known Troublemaker: A Life of Charlotte Charke* (London: Faber, 1988).

Morris, Joan, *Pope John VIII, an English Woman* (London: Vrai, 1985).

Mountfield, Anne, *Women and Education* (Hove: Wayland, 1990).

National Union of Women Workers, *Papers read at the Conference . . .* (London, 1903).

Neuburger, Verena, *Margery Kempe* [incl. Mary Astell, Hannah Woolley] (Bern, Switzerland: P. Lang, 1994).

Newcastle, Margaret, Duchess of, see *Letters and Poems* . . .

Newgate Calendar, vols. 1–4 (London [various publishers], *c*.1700–95).

Nicholas, Margaret, *The World's Wickedest Women* (London: Hamlyn, 1984).

[Nicholson, J.], *Lives of the Ancient Philosophers* (London: Nicholson, 1702).

Nightingale, Florence, *Suggestions for Thought to the Searchers after Truth* . . ., see Strachey, Ray.

Notes and Queries: A Medium of Intercommunication for Literary Men, General Readers. etc. (London: 'At the Office', 1872).

Nye-Starr, Kate, *A Self-Sustaining Woman* (Chicago, Ill.: Illinois Printing and Binding Co., 1888).

Ogilvie, M. B., *Women in Science* (Cambridge, Mass.: MIT Press, 1986).

Orwin, Thomas, *Boke His Surfeit in Love, with a farewel to the folies of his own phantasie* (1588).

Papworth, L. Wyatt and Zimmern, Dorothy, *The Occupations of Women According to the Census of England and Wales, 1911* (London: Women's Industrial Council, 1914).

Pardoe, Rosemary and Darroll, *The Female Pope* (Wellingborough: Crucible, 1988).

Pearson, Jacqueline, *The Prostituted Muse: Images of Women and Women Dramatists 1642–1737* (London: Harvester, 1988).

Peck, Annie, *A Search for the Apex of America* (New York: Dodd Mead, 1911).

Penguin Dictionary of Saints (ed. Donald Attwater) (Harmondsworth: Penguin, 1965).

Perry, Ruth, *The Celebrated Mary Astell* (Chicago, Ill.: University of Chicago Press, 1986).

Pfeiffer, Ida, *A Lady's Voyage Round the World* (London: Longman, Brown, 1852).

——, *Visit to the Holy Land, Egypt, and Italy* (London: Ingram, Cooke, 1852).

Philipps, Mrs, *et al.*, *Dictionary of Employments Open to Women* (London: Women's Institute, 1898).

Phillips, Patricia, *The Scientific Lady* . . . *1520–1918* (London: Weidenfeld and Nicolson, 1990).

Piccione, Peter, *Excursis III: The Status of Women in Ancient Egyptian Society* (www.library.nwu, 1995).

Pinchbeck, Ivy, *Women Workers and the Industrial Revolution 1750–1850* [1930] (London: Virago, 1981).

de Pizan, Christine (tr. A. Vigier), *Autobiography of a Medieval Woman* [a translation of *Le Livre de la Mutation*] (London: Minerva, 1996).

——, (tr. Earl Richards), *The Book of the City of Ladies* (London: Pan, 1983).

——, (tr. R. Brown-Grant), *Book of the City of Ladies* (Harmondsworth: Penguin, 1999).

——, (tr. S. Lawson), *The Treasure of the City of Ladies or the Book of the Three Virtues* (Harmondsworth: Penguin, 1985).

Plomer, Henry, *A Dictionary of the Booksellers and Printers . . . in England, Scotland and Ireland 1641–1667* (London: Bibliographical Society, 1907).

Prior, Mary (ed.), *Women in English Society 1500–1800* (London: Methuen, 1985).

Prout, Denton, *Petticoat Parade* [incl. Elizabeth Macarthur] (Adelaide, South Australia: Rigby, 1965).

Radcliffe, Mary Ann, *The Female Advocate Or, an Attempt to Recover the Rights of Woman from Male Usurpation* (London: Vernor and Hood, 1799).

Rae, Isobel, *The Strange Story of Dr. James Barry* (London: Longmans, Green, 1958).

Raven, S. and Weir, A., *Women in History* (London: Weidenfeld and Nicolson, 1981).

Rawlings, Philip, *Drunks, Whores, and Idle Apprentices* (London: Routledge, 1992).

Rendall, Jane, *Women in an Industrialising Society* (Oxford: Blackwell, 1990).

Roberts, Brian, *Those Bloody Women: Three Heroines of the Boer War* [incl. Lady Sarah Wilson] (London: Murray, 1991).

Robinson, Jane, *Parrot Pie for Breakfast: An Anthology of Women Pioneers* (Oxford: Oxford University Press, 1999).

——, *Unsuitable for Ladies: An Anthology of Women Travellers* (Oxford: Oxford University Press, 2001).

——, *Wayward Women: A Guide to Women Travellers* (Oxford: Oxford University Press, 2001).

Rogers, Cameron, *Gallant Ladies* [incl. Ann Bonny, Mary Read, Belle Starr] (New York: Harcourt, Brace, 1928).

Rose, June, *The Perfect Gentleman: The Remarkable Life of Dr James Miranda Barry* (London: Hutchinson, 1977).

Ross, I, *Ladies of the Press* [incl. Victoria Woodhull] (New York: Harper, 1936).

[Sampson, Deborah], *The Female Review* [1797] (Boston, Mass.: Wiggin and Lunt, 1866).

Sanderson, Elizabeth, *Women and Work in Eighteenth-century Edinburgh* (London: Macmillan, 1996).

Schneir, Miriam (ed.), *The Vintage Book of Historical Feminism* (London: Vintage, 1996).

Schreiner, Olive, *Women and Labour* [1911] (London: Virago, 1978).

van Schurman, Anna Maria (tr. J. Irwin), *Whether a Christian Woman Should be Educated* (Chicago, Ill.: University of Chicago Press, 1998).

——, *The Learned Maid; or, Whether a Maid may be a Scholar?* (London: Redmayne, 1659).

Seacole, Mary (ed. Ziggi Alexander and Audrey Dewjee), *Wonderful Adventures of Mrs Seacole in Many Lands* [1854] (Bristol: Falling Wall Press, 1984).

Seymour, Bruce, *Lola Montez: A Life* (New Haven, Conn.: Yale University Press, 1996).

Shaw, Stephanie, *What a Woman Ought to Be and to Do: Black Professional Women Workers* (Chicago, Ill.: University of Chicago Press, 1996).

Shore, David, *Hester Bateman* (London: W. H. Allen, 1959).

Singer, Kurt (ed.), *Three Thousand Years of Espionage* (New York: Prentice Hall, 1949).

Snell, Hannah, *The Female Soldier or the Surprising Life and Adventures . . .* (London: Walker, 1750).

Snow, Edward Rowe, *Women of the Sea* (New York: Dodd, Mead, 1963).

Spender, Dale, *Women of Ideas* (London: Routledge and Kegan Paul, 1982).

Spruill, Julia Cherry, *Women's Life and Work in the Southern Colonies* (Chapel Hill, NC: University of North Carolina Press, 1938).

Spufford, Margaret, *Small Books and Pleasant Histories: Popular Fiction . . . in Eighteenth-Century England* (London: Methuen, 1981).

Stanford, Peter, *The She-Pope: A Quest for . . . Pope Joan* (London: Heinemann, 1998).

Stark, Suzanne J., *Female Tars: Women Aboard Ship in the Age of Sail* (London: Constable, 1996).

Starke, Mariana, *Letters from Italy* (London: Phillips, 1800).

——, *Travels in Europe, for the use of Travellers on the Continent* (Paris: Galignani, 1839).

——, *Travels on the Continent* (London: Murray, 1820).

Stenton, Doris Mary, *The Englishwoman in History* (London: Allen and Unwin, 1957).

Stephens, Matthew, *Hannah Snell: The Secret Life of a Female Marine, 1723–1792* (London: Ship Street Press, 1997).

Stern, Madeleine, *We the Women: Career Firsts of Nineteenth-Century America* (New York: Schulte, 1962).

Stone, James, *Emily Faithfull* (Toronto: Meany, 1994).

Strachey, Ray, *The Cause: A Short History of the Women's Movement* [1928] (Bath: Chivers, 1974).

Strickland, Agnes, *Lives of the Queens of England* (London: Colburn, 1840–8).

Stuart, Marie, *Mary Seacole* (Bristol: C. and E. Bristol Adult Continuing Education, 1994).

Sweetman, David, *Women Leaders in African History* (London: Heinemann, 1984).

Swetnam, Joseph, *The Araignment of Lewd, idle, froward, and unconstant women* (London: Archer, 1616).

Talbot, Mary Anne, *The Life and Surprising Adventures* . . . (London: Kirby, 1809).

Teague, Frances, *Bathsua Makin* (Lewisburg, Penn.: Bucknell University Press, 1998).

The Literary Museum . . . Comprising Scarce and Curious Tracts [incl. Mary Astell] (London [Waldron], 1792).

Thompson, C. J. S., *The Quacks of Old London* (London: Brentano's, 1928).

Tickell, Crispin, *Mary Anning of Lyme Regis* (Lyme Regis: Philpot Museum, 1996).

Todd, Janet and Spearing, Elizabeth (eds), *Counterfeit Ladies* [Moll Cutpurse and Mary Carleton] (London: Pickering, 1994).

Todd, Janet, *The Secret Life of Aphra Behn* (London: André Deutsch, 1996).

Torrens, H., *Mary Anning* (Presidential Address published in the *British Journal for the History of Science*, vol. 28; London, 1995).

Trescott, Martha Moore (ed.), *Dynamos and Virgins Revisited: Women and Technological Change in History* (Metuchen, NJ: Scarecrow, 1979).

Underhill, Lois Beachy, *The Woman who Ran for President: The Many Lives of Victoria Woodhull* (New York: Penguin, 1995).

Universal British Directory (London: Stalker, Bridoake and Fell, 1790–8).

Usborne Book of Greek and Norse Legends (ed. Cheryl Evans), (London: Usborne, 1992).

Velasquez, Loreta Janeta (ed. C. J. Worthington), *The Woman in Battle* [1876] (New York: Arno Press, 1972).

Vicinus, Martha (ed.), *Suffer and Be Still: Women in the Victorian Age* (Bloomington, Ind.: Indiana University Press, 1972).

——, *Independent Women: Work and Community for Single Women 1850–1920* (London: Virago, 1985).

Vigier, A., *see* de Pizan, Christine.

Vizetelly, E., *The Warrior Woman* [incl. Christian Cavanagh, Phoebe Hessel, Loreta Velasquez and Lady Sarah Wilson] (London: Treherne, 1902).

Watherstone, Edward, *The Industrial Employment of Women* (London: Spottiswoode, 1878).

Wertheimer, Barbara Mayer, *We Were There: The Story of Working Women in America* (New York: Pantheon, 1977).

Wheelwright, Julie, *Amazons and Military Maids* (London: Pandora, 1989).

Whiting, Emma and Hough, Henry Beetle, *Whaling Wives* (Boston: Houghton and Mifflin, 1953).

'Why Are Women Redundant?', in *National Review*, vol. 14 (London, 1862).

Willard, Charity Cannon, *Christine de Pizan* (New York: Persea, 1984).

Wolcott, Robert, *A Woman in Steel – Rebecca Lukens* (Princeton, NJ: Princeton University Press, 1940).

Wollstonecraft, Mary (ed. Miriam Brody), *A Vindication of the Rights of Woman* [1792] (Harmondsworth: Penguin, 1985).

——, *Thoughts on the Education of Daughters* (London: Johnson, 1787).

[Woodhull, Victoria], *The Beecher-Tilton Scandal: A Complete History of the Case . . . as published in* Woodhull and Claflin's Weekly (Brooklyn, NY: Bancker, 1874).

——, and Claflin, Tennessee, *The Human Body . . . or, The Philosophy of Sociology . . . with other Essays* (London [privately printed], 1890).

——, *A Lecture on Constitutional Equality* (New York: Journeyman Printers' Co-operative, 1871).

Woolf, Virginia, *A Room of One's Own* [1928] (Harmondsworth: Penguin, 1945).

——, *The Death of the Moth* (London: Hogarth Press, 1942).

Woolley, Hannah, *The Gentlewoman's Companion* [1675] (Totnes: Prospect, 2001).

Wortley Montagu, Lady Mary, *The Works . . .* (London: Phillips, 1803).

Wright, Richardson, *Hawkers and Walkers in Early America* [incl. Anne Newport Royall] (Philadephia: Lippincott, 1927).

——, *Forgotten Ladies* [incl. Anne Newport Royall] (Philadelphia, Penn.: Lippincott, 1928).

Zanjani, Sally, *A Mine of Her Own: Women Prospectors in the American West 1850–1950* (Lincoln, Nebr.: University of Nebraska Press, 1997).

INDEX